Top Notes

Favel Parrett's

Past the Shallows

Study notes for Common Module:
Texts and Human Experiences
2019–2023 HSC

Bruce Pattinson

A
FIVE SENSES
PUBLICATION

Five Senses Education Pty Ltd
2/195 Prospect Highway
Seven Hills 2147
New South Wales
Australia

Pattinson, Bruce
Top Notes – Past the Shallows
ISBN 978-1-76032-216-8

CONTENTS

TOP NOTES SERIES

This series has been created to assist HSC students of English in their understanding of set texts. Top Notes are easy to read, providing analysis of issues and discussion of important ideas contained in the texts.

Particular care has been taken to ensure that students are able to examine each text in the context of the module it has been allocated to.

Each text generally includes:

- Notes on the specific module
- Plot summary
- Character analysis
- Setting
- Thematic concerns
- Language studies
- Essay questions and a modelled response
- Other textual material
- Study practice questions
- Useful quotes

We have covered the areas we feel are important for students in their study of *Texts and Human Experiences* for their Common Module. I am sure you will find these Top Notes useful in your studies of English.

Bruce Pattinson
Series Editor

COMMON MODULE: TEXTS AND HUMAN EXPERIENCES

"It is quite possible—overwhelmingly probable, one might guess—
that we will always learn more about human life and personality
from novels than from scientific psychology"

NOAM CHOMSKY

What is the Common Module?

The Common Module set for the 2019–23 HSC is *Texts and Human Experiences*. It is compulsory to study this topic as prescribed by NESA and it is common to all three English courses. Remember: you will be learning how texts reveal individual and collective human experiences. There are no right or wrong answers in this module – it is about how you see and interpret material and engage with it.

In the Common Module you will be analysing one prescribed text and a range of short texts that are related to the idea of human experiences. You will analyse texts not only to investigate the ideas they present about this area but also how they convey these ideas. This means you will be looking closely at the techniques a composer uses to represent his / her messages and shape meaning. You will also be looking at relationships between texts in regard to the experiences you explore. Overall, you will become an expert on texts and the human experience — that is, the different notions people have about human experience and the various ways composers manipulate techniques to communicate their ideas about it.

Specifically you will look at one set text from the following list.

- Doerr, Anthony, *All the Light We Cannot See*
- Lohrey, Amanda, *Vertigo*
- Orwell, George, *Nineteen Eighty-Four*
- Parrett, Favel, *Past the Shallows*
- Dobson, Rosemary 'Young Girl at a Window', 'Over the Hill', 'Summer's End', 'The Conversation', 'Cock Crow', 'Amy Caroline', 'Canberra Morning'
- Slessor, Kenneth 'Wild Grapes', 'Gulliver', 'Out of Time', 'Vesper-Song of the Reverend Samuel Marsden', 'William Street', 'Beach Burial'
- Harrison, Jane, *Rainbow's End*
- Miller, Arthur, *The Crucible*
- Shakespeare, William, *The Merchant of Venice*
- Winton, Tim, *The Boy Behind the Curtain* Chapters: 'Havoc: A Life in Accidents', 'Betsy', 'Twice on Sundays', 'The Wait and the Flow', 'In the Shadow of the Hospital', 'The Demon Shark', 'Barefoot in the Temple of Art'
- Yousafzai, Malala & Lamb, Christina, *I am Malala*
- Daldry, Stephen, *Billy Elliot*
- O'Mahoney, Ivan, *Go Back to Where You Came From –* Series 1, Episodes 1, 2 and 3 and *The Response*
- Walker, Lucy, *Waste Land*

NESA has mandated that students must study a related text as part of the common module, and that this should be part of their in-school assessment. However there is NO LONGER a requirement to write about a related text in the HSC examination itself.

WHAT DOES NESA REQUIRE FOR THE COMMON MODULE?

The NESA documentation of the Common Module: Texts and Human Experiences states that students:

- deepen their understanding of how texts represent individual and collective human experiences;

- examine how texts represent human qualities and emotions associated with, or arising from, these experiences;

- appreciate, explore, interpret, analyse and evaluate the ways language is used to shape these representations in a range of texts in a variety of forms, modes and media;

- explore how texts may give insight into the anomalies, paradoxes and inconsistencies in human behaviour and motivations, inviting the responder to see the world differently, to challenge assumptions, ignite new ideas or reflect personally;

- may also consider the role of storytelling throughout time to express and reflect particular lives and cultures;

- by responding to a range of texts, further develop skills and confidence using various literary devices, language concepts, modes and media to formulate a considered response to texts;

- study one prescribed text and a range of short texts that provide rich opportunities to further explore representations of human experiences illuminated in texts;

- make increasingly informed judgements about how aspects of these texts, for example, context, purpose, structure, stylistic and grammatical features, and form shape meaning;

- select one related text and draw from personal experience to make connections between themselves, the world of the text and their wider world;

- by responding and composing throughout the module, further develop a repertoire of skills in comprehending, interpreting and analysing complex texts;

- examine how different modes and media use visual, verbal and/or digital language elements;

- communicate ideas using figurative language to express universal themes and evaluative language to make informed judgements about texts;

- further develop skills in using metalanguage, correct grammar and syntax to analyse language and express a personal perspective about a text

If this is what is required by NESA, we need to examine the concept of human experience carefully so we can adequately respond in these ways. I would recommend that you read the complete document which is on the NESA web site and can be downloaded in Word or Adobe. Understanding this document is an important step in handling the textual material within the guidelines required — remember you are reading for a purpose and should make notes and highlight ideas as you read so that you can develop these ideas later.

UNDERSTANDING THE COMMON MODULE

What are Human Experiences?

The concept of Human Experiences is at the heart of the Common Module.

Human Experiences are experiences of individuals or a group of people (eg a family, society, or nation) in life. There are a very wide range of human experiences which include but go beyond this list:

- feelings or reactions (momentary or long term): love, hate, anger, joy, fear, disgust
- key milestones or stages: birth, childhood, adulthood, marriage, divorce, death
- culture, belonging and identity
- conformity and rebellion
- innocence and guilt, justice
- freedom and repression
- education, vocation, work, sport, leisure
- attraction to a person, idea, group or cause
- opposition to an idea, cause, political system
- religious faith or belief
- extreme events such as an earthquake, avalanche, tsuanami
- regular events such as walking, eating, singing, dancing, discussing ideas.

The word *experience* seems innately connected to the human condition and it is something we have each day whether a mundane experience that is repetitive, or something new and dramatic which offers challenges and rewards. Experiences can vary greatly in their impact on individuals, groups and countries. One example might be a war that is a negative experience for a whole population while we may experience the wonder of medicine with a new vaccine for a deadly disease that saves millions of people. We need to note that the module asks for 'experiences' ...we are a combination of different experiences and each has a varying impact. One person's problem is another's challenge depending on perspective, skill set, previous experience and ability.

Experiences are widespread and often shared: this is why people tell their stories and these shared experiences form part of our cultural heritage. These experiences often inform, warn and teach across entire cultural groups and many stories are shared across cultures.

DEFINING HUMAN EXPERIENCES

Now let's attempt to define what human experiences are and shape them into a more coherent and easily understood framework so we can begin our investigation at a basic level of understanding before moving into more complex analysis and looking at how the texts illuminate our understanding of the term.

Dictionary.com defines the term **experience** as:

noun

1. a particular instance of personally encountering or undergoing something:

2. the process or fact of personally observing, encountering, or undergoing something:

3. the observing, encountering, or undergoing of things generally as they occur in the course of time:
   to learn from experience; the range of human experience.

4. knowledge or practical wisdom gained from what one has observed, encountered, or undergone, e.g. *a man of experience.*

5. *Philosophy.* the totality of the cognitions given by perception; all that is perceived, understood, and remembered.

verb
(used with object), **experienced, experiencing.**

6. to have experience of; meet with; undergo; feel,
   e.g. *to experience nausea.*

7. to learn by experience.

idiom

8. **experience religion**, to undergo a spiritual conversion by which one gains or regains faith in God.

Obviously there are a number of definitions according to context, but all are applicable to our study in some shape or form, as the range of human experience is so vast. The search for 'new experience' has driven much of the development of people, groups, cultures and nations over past millennia. New experiences are always met with excitement and often trepidation as to what change they might bring.

Think historically about how people have reacted to change. It can cause great upheavals in society, with violent reactions while other changes brought through various experiences are welcomed and may change how people live and comprehend the world. Experiences affect us emotionally in many cases rather than logically and when we respond emotionally, behaviours become unpredictable. This causes the paradoxes, anomalies and inconsistencies mentioned in the rubric. If we were logical beings the world would be an easier place, but probably more boring.

These definitions all point to the fact that memory is the key to experience. The experience is stored in memory and drawn upon when the circumstances are repeated or closely mimicked so we can deal with them — hopefully better than on the initial experience.

Experiences can come in many ways and the synonyms listed below for experience help us to understand the concept even further. They assist in defining how an experience can arise:

Synonyms

actions

background

contacts

involvement

know-how

maturity

participation

patience

practice

reality

sense

skill

struggle

training

understanding

wisdom

acquaintances

actuality

caution

combat

doings

empiricism

evidence

existences

exposures

familiarity

intimacy

inwardness

judgment

observation

perspicacity

practicality

proofs

savoir-faire

seasonings

sophistication

strife

trials

worldliness

forebearance

http://www.thesaurus.com/browse/experience?s=t

These synonyms show partly the vast array of words that our language has created around this concept, and also shows how important it is in the human psyche. We, as humans, want to experience. Now we will look at some examples of experiences and examine how they can have an impact. It is also important to remember that experiences do not have to be positive. You might experience a huge problem, a bereavement, a car accident, an unwelcome relationship or something totally bizarre that rocks your world. There can be a more opaque side to any experience that may need to be addressed.

The whole aim of this Common Module is to examine the text closely but also relate it to the concept of human experiences and decide how examining it in this way enables us to better understand both the text and the concept of humanity.

It is important that you unpack what each text you study shows you about human experiences and what ideas / themes arise from those experiences. Formulate your own ideas about the text.

Read the NESA Stage 6 document called *English Stage 6: Annotations of selected texts prescribed for the Higher School Certificate 2019–23* (see *www.educationstandards.nsw.edu.au*) for the set text you are studying. This document offers insights into the way each particular text should be examined by outlining key ideas and areas for clarification.

Human experiences and ways of experiencing vary due to individual circumstance and these experiences can change many things about individual lives, communities and the world. When we examine the concept of human experience in relation to a text, we need to examine the assumptions or biases we bring to it as well as how experiencing the text itself may change us and how we view things. The text may challenge and confront how we view the human experience or we may have preconceived ideas that make it more difficult for this to happen.

Students can also think about their own 'personal experience to make connections between themselves, the world of the text and their wider world.' Examining and enjoying any text is an experience in itself but it is what we take away from the text and apply that is the crucial aspect. That is not to say that every text will be enjoyed or offer a human experience that is significant either positively or negatively. Some texts may not personally engage you and that is fine. This is especially so when you begin to look for other related material that links to *Texts and Human Experiences*. We recommend that you find examples of texts that link but also personally appeal to you so that you can relate empathetically with them.

Individual Human Experiences

The idea of personal experiences is a popular and pervasive concept, especially in the literature of many cultures. Recording personal experiences as a means of sharing wisdom or more mundane daily tasks is part of human nature and we record and relate these experiences frequently. Experiences are recorded and relayed in many ways. We tell oral stories in both anecdotal and formal ways, we write, draw, sing and photograph our way into history (or not). Look at the proliferation of social media in this current century as people record their daily, even hourly, experiences for all to see. We record the most trivial details of our lives for likes and followers while the real world passes us by. Human experiences affect us on a daily basis and some experiences influence our lives and the way we live them.

Individuals seek out experiences in a variety of ways. Some seek more and more extreme experiences to test themselves against the world. Others limit their experiences. A lot of people prefer the familiar and don't actively seek new experiences. Individuals, it must be remembered, also see experiences in different ways and the same experience may have a very different impact on individuals. The one thing we can be certain about is that experiences are part of humanity and even the most limited of us have them. Many of these experiences also come from interaction with others and as noted we also like to share these experiences.

Experiences are what define us in many ways and are what makes us human.

We are going to look at four specific ways that experiences can influence us as people over the next few pages. These are physical, psychological, emotional and intellectual experiences and many experiences are a combination of these.

Physical Experience

The concept of a physical experience is tied into the human experience and part of the collective experience as well. Individuals seek physical experiences to test themselves against nature and other individuals often as part of trials and rituals, for example being integrated into a community. In modern times individuals have sought to test themselves with extreme sports and explorations into the harshest conditions and even space. Physical experiences can also change the way we see the world and others because of the chemical changes these experiences have on our bodies and mind. Physical experiences are often challenges and part of the experience is overcoming adversity. These physical challenges are often celebrated, as in the case of sports, but can also offer challenges if the experience is a negative one such as an accident or disease. Physical experiences are also often quite public and thus have permeated our societies in both their execution and how they are perceived. These physical experiences, even if experienced vicariously, have become popular across cultures and celebrated. Think of examples for yourself but most competitive sports offer examples.

Bruce Lee extends the concept of the physical experience into all aspects of life and that's what we will look at next in our analysis of human experiences –

'If you always put limits on everything you do, physical or anything else, it will spread into your work and into your life. There are no limits. There are only plateaus, and you must not stay there, you must go beyond them.'

Psychological Experience

The idea of a psychological experience is tied into many of the abstract ideas that people experience and can lead to a discussion of what is normal psychology. From the earliest times humans have attempted to alter their psychology through a number of experiences. On a simple level this can be a drug that changes the person's or group's perspective on reality. Examples of this might be alcohol or marijuana but cultural groups also use various substances to share group experiences. This can be seen in Native American cultures with *peyote*. In more modern times prescription drugs that are mood altering have been used to minimise the symptoms of psychiatric illnesses such as depression, and these mood altering drugs are common and legal. Others attempt to alter their psychology by seeing specialists in this area while others act out their condition leading to social and criminal issues. When discussing the human experience, psychology is a key issue and will form a part of most studies of experience. When taken too far this search for a new psychological experience can be harmful eg. an addiction.

Carl Jung, the famous psychologist, comments on the problems of addiction for human experiences, stating clearly that excess can be an issue:

"Every form of addiction is bad, no matter whether the narcotic be alcohol, morphine or idealism."

Emotional Experience

According to the psychologist, Robert Plutchik, there are eight basic emotions:

- **Fear** — feeling afraid.
- **Anger** — feeling angry. A stronger word for anger is rage.
- **Sadness** — feeling sad. Other words are sorrow, grief (a stronger feeling, for example when someone has died) or **depression** (feeling sad for a long time without any external cause). Some people think depression is a different emotion.
- **Joy** — feeling happy. Other words are happiness, gladness.
- **Disgust** — feeling something is wrong or nasty
- **Trust** — a positive emotion; admiration is stronger; **acceptance** is weaker
- **Anticipation** — in the sense of looking forward positively to something which is going to happen. **Expectation** is more neutral; **dread** is more negative.

https://simple.wikipedia.org/wiki/List_of_emotions

Emotions are the strongest drivers of human experience and form lasting aspects of any experience. Think about breaking up with someone you love and the emotions that drive behaviours in this situation. People have all sorts of extreme behaviours under the influence of emotions and these experiences are often the ones recorded and those which influence us most. Think about the role emotions play in our lives and the range of emotions from the list above. Consider how much emotions affect our life experiences, how they influence our decisions which decide our experiences and on a higher level consider how they affect the decisions which may seriously impact our experiences, such as politicians going to war.

Intellectual Experience

The concept of an intellectual experience is linked to decisions and experiences we have based on analysis and logic rather than the emotional choices referred to in the previous section. These intellectual experiences have changed the way we live and how we have seen our world. These experiences have affected the way we as humans have altered our world to suit our needs and lead to all the great advances in human society and thus experiences. Changes in our ideas, beliefs etc. alter the way we interact with the world and often these intellectual changes come at great cost.

Think of the time in Europe when the Church dominated and stopped scientific advances by calling them heresy/witchcraft. Open societies are more open to new ideas and this is what has hastened the pace of intellectual experiences as dominant ideologies fall away. Intellectual advances may not have the excitement that the other types produce but perhaps they have a more lasting impact on people, societies and the world in general. Ideas are powerful experiences and people hold beliefs strongly.

Immanuel Kant stated that:

> *"experience without theory is blind, but theory without experience is mere intellectual play."*

Consider this statement in the light of what we have learnt about human experiences. Are they a combination of many factors or can we isolate experiences into simple forms?

What exactly is a human experience?

The titular question reminds us of the old brainteaser: "If a tree falls in a forest and no one is around to hear it, does it make a sound?"

There are two classic responses to this. The more Platonically-minded would say the tree always makes a sound when it falls in the forest. We don't have to be there to hear it; we can imagine the sound of a tree falling in the forest, based on memory of such an event or on the recording of such an event. We know that sound is just vibrating air, and it's safe to say that air always vibrates in response to a tree falling, or a bear growling, or a cicada singing, whether we are there to hear it or not.

The second answer is a more post-structuralist response: the sound doesn't occur on its own; it needs a human ear to be heard. Therefore, if there is no human in the forest to hear the tree fall, then there is no sound. This automatically implies that "experience" of anything requires the presence of a human being, which means there is no such thing as an experience that *isn't* human.

Animal rights activists – or anyone with a beloved pet – would almost certainly reject this notion because it prioritises humans and relegates all other species to a lower class of being: an attitude that most would agree has gotten the human race into an awful lot of environmental trouble over the last 200 years of industrialisation.

In his article (*What is an Experience?*), my learned colleague Paul Hartley describes experience in its most basic form, as "the perception of something else" and "ultimately information about what we have perceived." But does this make it particularly human? Dogs and cats perceive things. Insects perceive things. You could even say that plants perceive things, such as the direction from which the sun is shining. Perception is the most basic of life's survival tools for all manner of flora and fauna.

In her brief but cogent disquisition on the subject (*What is Human?*), another of my learned colleagues, Nadine Hare, asserts that to be human is a social construct. Hartley builds on that notion by suggesting that culture affects experience when we start to share it, because "the words, associations, and priorities we attach to the shared experience define how we understand the world we live in."

Hare rightly points out that this world is increasingly dominated by consumerism, which has distorted what it means to be human by excluding all of the attributes and qualities that "make people people." Calling us consumers reduces our experiences to mere transactions. It defines human experience within the narrow confines of the purchase funnel and has little interest in anything that isn't a purchase driver.

Perhaps the field of commerce is where the experiential rubber most emphatically meets the road. Unlike mere perception, commerce is a uniquely human experience. It has mediated, automated, and dominated the human agenda to the point where we are defined by what we buy and little else. Commerce has invaded the non-profit spheres of government, health, and education, imposing its own priorities and principles on these institutions in the expectation that they will behave more like businesses. And even though business still strives to appeal to the so-called masses, it prioritises the pursuit of individual wealth, and in so doing, not only inhibits the desire for shared experience but unravels the social fabric historically woven by the democratic tradition.

As if in response, that social fabric is being re-woven by our networks. As Hare asserts, "humans both produce technology and are produced through technology." Experience is shared more now than it ever has been because the experiential platform – i.e., that very human invention called the internet – is in place to facilitate it like never before, and on a global scale.

This sharing capability reintroduces all of those things that "make people people" back into the conversation – whether commercial or political. What "makes people people" is messy, unpredictable, emotional, and complex. Most of what makes us human has no place in the experiential confines of the purchase funnel, and defies any of our attempts to place it there.

The challenge for us as a species is to embrace this new capacity for sharing to keep the agendas of our hegemonic institutions – whether commercial or political – from defining what makes an experience human. A post-consumer business strategy might be one that, as Hare hopes, will "expand our view of people to include the complex and dynamic social, cultural, gendered, spiritual and racialised beings that they are." Maybe then will our shared human experience truly become, as Hartley asserts, the glue that holds us all together as human beings.

Will Novosedlik
MISC magazine

https://miscmagazine.com/what-is-a-human-experience/

This article appeared in the September 2014 edition of MISC magazine. Can you relate to what the article says about human experiences? Do human experiences depend on perception? Does the experience of anything require the presence of a human as experiencer (para 3)? Can the ideas of experience be extended to include perception by plants or animals? Hartley's idea is that "shared human experience" is "the glue that holds us all together as human beings". Is this an oversimplification?

The Impact of Human Experiences

Human experiences have impacts on many levels. On an individual level, we can have changes in our assumptions about the world and people around us; we can ingest new ideas and have these open new vistas of productivity and performance. We can also reflect and build on these experiences to ensure that they are even more meaningful to our lives. Behaviours towards others and the way we respond to the world can manifest themselves in new and different responses. An example might be that through adverse experiences we can build resilience so that the next negative experience isn't as traumatic and we accept it for what it is. Experiences also teach us new behaviours on a very physical level — if you burn yourself once on a flame you learn not to do it again (hopefully).

The impact of human experiences can also be shared in groups and societies. Firstly, let's examine some group dynamics that can be affected by human experiences. Groups share experiences and adapt and develop behaviours that impact on the group as a whole. Think about the notorious 'bonding' sessions sporting teams have that unite them in a common goal. Think about the behaviours of various gangs in our society. We see plenty of examples of this on American television where gangs based on ethnicity and social groupings form specific sets of behaviours that impact on how they interact with each other and the world. These groupings carry assumptions about how they see the world and respond to it. For example, they may have generally negative reactions to law enforcement and this is ingrained into their codes of behaviour. They are suspicious of the world and the people in it — dividing them up into threats, the law and victims. These behaviours are often reinforced by group experiences such as the initiation rituals which are integral to membership.

Often the impact of these behaviours is to perpetuate stereotypes that then categorise the individuals within these groups. The graphic I have included here shows a stereotypical gang member with the suspicious gaze, ubiquitous hoody and scruffy look. These stereotypes reject new ideas and maintain assumptions about the world, often to the detriment of their members. The experiences they have reinforce their own stereotypical way of viewing anything outside the safety of the group and the cycle continues. Of course, other groups have more positive impacts and see the world as a  very different place and their experiences are designed to be positive interactions. Think about groups such as Rotary who are constructive in the community. Other groups have specialty interests such as Animal Welfare, Surf Lifesaving and charities.

Normal social interactions impact groups and individuals, but it takes a major event to alter the behaviours of whole societies, especially so in the modern world where societies are large in scale. Earlier in human history smaller experiences could alter the behaviour of societies as they were insignificant in size compared to modern ones. We often fail to remember that many of these ancient societies' behaviours were impacted by superstition, religions and cultural habituation. The modern society as we know it is only a recent phenomenon. Just a few hundred years ago with church rule people were forced to think in a specific

way and punished for not adhering to a theological culture. Think of the Spanish Inquisition, the imprisonment of Galileo and other such restrictions on freedom of thought; scientific breakthroughs were hidden or declared witchcraft. Even recently the world has seen societies kept repressed by failed ideologies. The brutality of such regimes has left deep scars on the social psyche of nations as they try to recover. This has had an impact on the human experiences of whole populations, and societies respond accordingly.

One example might be at the conclusion of the Communist regime in East Germany when the Berlin Wall was destroyed as a visual symbol of the new-found freedom of a whole population of people who had been repressed for decades by a brutal and ever-present regime. Many citizens who had grown up in this system, where you could 'disappear' without trial or real evidence, found the idea that you could express yourself incredible. Many of the

East Germans couldn't believe that this freedom was real and that the Stasi (the secret police) were gone.

Other experiences can affect societies in extreme ways. Think about wars and the impact they have on civilian populations.

Climatic events such as earthquakes change the way that people behave and respond to situations. Catastrophic flooding occurred in the US city of New Orleans in 2005. The US President's response to help was not immediate and the national administration was severely criticised for lack of effective action.

Societies also respond to perceived problems such as pollution. In 1989 the oil tanker Exxon Valdez ran aground in Prince William Sound, Alaska with disastrous results. The effects of this event are still being experienced thirty years later.

Societies can be divided, as we saw with the election of Donald Trump in the United States of America and the reaction of the Political Left.

The impact of human experiences on societies can be quite dramatic, as we have seen, while other experiences (such as an election) can go by without a murmur from societies, no matter who wins. As a last thought before we move on you should also consider the impact of the media on societies in the modern world, and how they influence individuals, societies and the development of ideas.

Problems With Human Behaviour

So far, we have discussed the impact of human experiences on behaviour. Now we can begin to develop some more complex judgements and understandings about the impact of those experiences on human behaviours. In simplistic terms it could be assessed as:

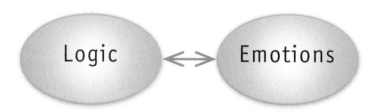

These two opposites on the continuum certainly shape the manner in which we see incidents and how they affect the experience. For instance, if someone you love has no interest in you, it creates a very different reaction to someone you don't care about having no interest in you. It is generally agreed that humans respond more strongly with emotion than they do with logic. Often, it is only through time and reflection that we can understand how an experience has changed and/or altered the manner in which we see a situation or individual.

The Role of Storytelling in Human Experiences

Storytelling has been part of the human experience since 'people' began communicating and it is a method used to convey information and experience as well as be entertaining. Earliest myths were all oral and then people began to write down stories so they weren't lost in time. From this, various theories have developed around storytelling and one is the 'monomyth', which is a template across cultures for storytelling. Let's have a look at this below.

'In narratology and comparative mythology, the monomyth, or the hero's journey, is the common template of a broad category of tales that involve a hero who goes on an adventure, and in a decisive crisis wins a victory, and then comes home changed or transformed.

The concept was introduced in *The Hero with a Thousand Faces* (1949) by Joseph Campbell, who described the basic narrative pattern as follows:

> "A hero ventures forth from the world of common day into a region of supernatural wonder: fabulous forces are there encountered and a decisive victory is won: the hero comes back from this mysterious adventure with the power to bestow boons on his fellow man."

Campbell and other scholars, such as Erich Neumann, describe narratives of Gautama Buddha, Moses, and Christ in terms of the monomyth. Critics argue that the concept is too broad or general to be of much use in comparative mythology. Others say that the hero's journey is only a part of the monomyth; the other part is a sort of different form, or colour, of the hero's journey.

https://en.wikipedia.org/wiki/Hero%27s_journey

Storytelling in History and its Purpose in Human Experience

Storytelling in oral form was accompanied by some theatrics to make the stories as entertaining as possible. Many of the early narratives were based upon religious ceremonies and stories of the creation of the earth and people(s). As time moved on, these stories were accompanied by dance, music and / or theatre and often were part of lengthy rituals, often taking days. These stories were designed to bring meaning to people's lives by explaining their own existence and the purpose / meaning of life in a time when life expectancy was short and entertainment was scarce. Of course stories were also recorded as these experiences were significant to all people and these stories run across all cultures. Before writing, stories were recorded in pictures such as cave art, in tattoo designs on skin and in designs such as rock piles and the giant carved heads of Easter Island.

Writing changed the manner in which stories were told and many of the old oral traditions were lost, barely being kept alive by specialists. Stories began to travel across cultural and national boundaries on whatever surface could be created. Papyrus, bones, pottery, skins, paper and in more modern times film, video and digital storage have changed, over time, the way in which stories of human experience have been told and shared. Content evolved from myth, fable and legend to history, personal narratives and commentary. Modern narrative form often has an educational or didactic element and can drift into propaganda. Stories of self-revelation can be instructive and give audiences the opportunity to apply learning to individual lives, whereas historically narrative was used in this way for societies and groups as a whole. In recent times narratives have become interactive and audiences can choose how the narrative unfolds.

Whatever form the story takes we all have a seemingly innate need for narratives to make sense of our lives. They either confirm our world view or alter our world view depending on the experience they convey and the experiences that we bring to the narrative. We need to remember that narratives are important to human experience and have been significant since the beginning of time.

The Text as an Experience

The concept of the text as an experience is one area to consider as we look at *Texts and Human Experiences*. Reading or viewing the text is an experience in itself and when we do this we bring our own history (experiences) to the text and this helps shape our understanding.

Think about the personal perspective that you bring to a text. What are some of your experiences that might influence how you read a particular text? Some texts, especially personal narratives of trial and tribulation or loss, can be confronting to some audiences and bring back strong opinions or emotions. Many texts attempt to do this as they convey a particular point of view about the world.

Does what you bring to the text affect what you learn from that text? We also need to delve into how the narrative experience is conveyed and how this in turn impacts upon the manner in which the story is received by audiences across different cultures. For example, Western films where heroes fight Islamic terrorism may well be viewed very differently by audiences in Western democracies and Islamic countries. Even seemingly innocuous narratives like the movie 'The Red Pill' which is about men's rights and created by a woman, has caused a polarisation of views wherever it has been shown. Strong personal experiences and viewpoints certainly bring their own understandings to texts.

Questions for Texts and Human Experiences

- Define the module in your own words.
- How are people connected by shared experiences?
- How might physical experience(s) change the way you respond to the world?
- How do you think a person's context and prior experiences shape how they perceive the world?
- Are experiences unique or do prior experiences have an impact on a current experience and way of seeing life?
- What is positive about human experiences?
- Discuss what is negative about human experiences.
- To what extent does experience shape the way we see other people and/or groups?
- Is an individual's culture part of their experience or is it something else?
- Is it possible not to have any meaningful experiences at all?
- Why do people tell stories?
- What do you think you might learn from a narrative?

THE AUTHOR

Favel Parrett is an Australian author who lived in Hobart for seven years early in her life and this is where the geography and feel of the novel come from. This authenticity can be read in the descriptions of the coast, the lifestyles and attitudes of the people that she includes in her novel and in the way that the novel has the sea as a living force. Now living in Melbourne she has completed a second novel *When the Night Comes*. The novel you are studying, *Past the Shallows* has won many awards including being shortlisted for the Miles Franklin Award.

There are several websites that you can garner information about her and these shed some light on the workings of the novel and novelist. The primary site is her own:

http://www.favelparrett.com.au/

Some others include:

https://en.wikipedia.org/wiki/Favel_Parrett – the Wikipedia site which has links to other areas including two reviews of the novel.

At *http://www.smh.com.au/entertainment/books/past-the-shallows-20110610-1fw44.html* Juliet Hughes says of the novel in her concluding comments;

> 'This is an impressive debut. Parrett's writing has a real voice, with power to evoke feeling, place and character. She is capable of refreshing narrative clarity, yet at other times surprises with an intense lyricism that is never self-indulgent. Everyone is put to the test — pushed to the edge physically and spiritually in a series of events and

revelations that affect not only the characters but also the reader. This book is that rare thing, a finely crafted literary novel that is genuinely moving and full of heart.'

Australian readers will notice the particular language of the characters and the settings but the novel transcends this and with what are called colloquially 'universal themes' the novel explores many modern social issues. Reviews of the novel were generally positive and most conclude like this;

> 'This is a beautifully written book. The spare prose carries the story like a swiftly moving current, but makes space for small moments of connection, too – Miles discovering Aunty Jean's hoard of unused baby clothes; Harry buying a tin of tea for George. The climax, when it comes, is as breathtaking as it is inevitable. This is a heartbreaker of a novel, and bodes well for this young writer's future.'

http://newtownreviewofbooks.com.au/2012/02/28/favel-parrett-past-the-shallows/

This is a contemporary novel and an accessible one that offers plenty in terms of human experiences.

CONTEXT

Some of the context of the novel has been mentioned when we looked at the author but here we can develop some of those ideas. The 'Australianness' of the novel is clear, not just from the Tasmanian setting but in the manner of the characterisations. The heavy drinking father who heads straight to the pub after fishing is a stereotype but a realistic one of that type of working class man. We see the struggle of the few characters in the novel as they are low in socio-economic status and the jealousy aimed at Mr Roberts for breaking out of that poverty cycle. This 'tall poppy' concept is typically Australian and the 'politics of envy' is alive and well in Tassie.

Despite this we see the warmth and decency of the average person with George helping Harry and Miles despite his own problems and handicaps. We also see Stuart's mum who is a kind, loving woman who doesn't say much but acts positively as she works to raise her own boy. The boys themselves are very loving and sensible despite the harsh upbringing at the hands of a bitter father whose obligation to the bank is another millstone that many Australians would comprehend.

The final part of the context is the abalone fishing which has been touched on. Below is an article from *Bookbrowse* that contains the basics of abalone fishing and it emphasises the rewards and dangers so we get a good understanding of what the men are doing and perhaps why they are so hard and under pressure.

'In *Past the Shallows*, the boys' father is an abalone fisherman off the southern Tasmanian coast. Abalone are gastropods—single-shelled molluscs—similar to snails, but with a more flattened shell. Other than their size and respiratory pores—large holes near the edge—their outer shell is often unremarkable. However, their inner iridescent appearance is prized by collectors and used for mother-of-pearl jewellery. Primarily, abalone are hunted and sold as a culinary delicacy. Although abalone farms also provide demanding consumers with these tasty molluscs, wild abalone are more highly valued. In Australia, the largest abalone producing country in the world, there are two types: blacklip and the more valuable greenlip. China is the largest importer of Australian abalone and an increase in demand has led to greater profits and therefore greater risks have been taken to procure them.

To look at an abalone, it is difficult to imagine any danger associated with fishing for them. It's not like they could attack a diver. Their only protection is their large strong shell and a powerful "foot" muscle that enables them to cling tightly to rocks. And yet, diving for abalone can be an extremely dangerous endeavour; especially in southern Australia where *Past the Shallows* takes place.'

https://www.bookbrowse.com/mag/btb/index.cfm/book_number/3049/
past-the-shallows#btb

PLOT OUTLINE

The father is an abalone fisherman but is angry and not coping

Novel's setting in Tasmania and three brothers introduced

Joe, the eldest, doesn't live at home. Miles works the boat

Harry, the youngest, goes to the Hobart Show and finds $20

Aunty Jean cries at lunch over Harry's dead mother.

Dad is under pressure because of the debt and the past

Harry meets George Fuller's dog

Joe and Miles go surfing and Joe tells he is leaving.

Martin is injured by the shark and the catch is lost

Harry now meets George and they share tea

Mr Roberts 'rescues' Miles and warns him to leave

Aunty Jean cuts the boys hair and things are getting worse

Granddad's house is cleaned

Miles finds the shark tooth

Harry talks about the accident

Miles fights with Gary Bones

Miles and Joe argue about the accident

Harry and George go fishing

The father is drinking heavily

Harry and George pick fruit and are now friends

The Fisheries officers come looking for 'Steven Curran' and Harry is worried

Miles goes to Grandad's and thinks of his life

Miles and Joe surf the 'Bone Yard'

Joe says he is leaving tomorrow. Miles wants to get away too

Jeff and Dad drink for two days

The boys retreat to George's after Miles is struck. Miles dreams of his mother

Miles takes Harry to Stuart's house

Miles goes home and cleans

Dad brings back fish and chips

Miles has to go fishing again

Harry buys the tea at the shop

Harry goes to George's and falls asleep

Harry is nearly run over by his dad

Harry is forced to go fishing on the boat

They head out to the 'Rocks' a lonely spot

The engine stops and the air is cut to dad and Jeff

They make it to deck but are sick. Dad gets angry

Miles is attacked by dad and is nearly drowned

Harry tries to save Miles

Dad's role in the accident is revealed and he pushes Harry overboard

Miles tries to save Harry

Miles is rescued and Harry is found drowned by George

Joe and Miles plan to get away

SUMMARY WITH COMMENTARY

Introductory Quote

The initial quote from Admiral D'Entrecasteaux begins with the idea of the wildness of the Tasmanian coast. He was a genuine historical figure:

> Antoine Raymond Joseph de Bruni d'Entrecasteaux (8 November 1737 – 21 July 1793) was a French naval officer, explorer and colonial governor. He is perhaps best known for his exploration of the Australian coast in 1792, while searching for the La Pérouse expedition.
>
> https://en.wikipedia.org/wiki/Antoine_Bruni_d%27Entrecasteaux

The significance of the quote will come to light as the narrative progresses.

Prologue

The prologue links the quote and the narrative with the 'black and cold sea' which hides the 'Treasure' that is the abalone. Abalone are shellfish like a giant oyster and are quite valuable in the fishery. More information about abalone fishing in Tasmania can be found at:

http://dpipwe.tas.gov.au/sea-fishing-aquaculture/recreational-fishing/abalone-fishing

The novel isn't divided into chapters but is written in a more episodic manner. For convenience I have numbered these and given a page number so you can find the relevant section quickly and easily.

1. (p1)

Here Parrett gives us the orientation to the novel, introducing three brothers; Joe, Miles and Harry. The foreshadowing of the conclusion is clear when Harry feels the ocean 'would be there always, right inside him.' The two older boys give Harry a treasure hunt to keep him occupied while they surf. He finds an old midden, thinks of death and heads back along the beach. Harry waits for his brothers and when Joe, the oldest, finally comes in they share some food and wait for Miles.

2. (p7)

Miles is now working on the 'Lady Ida' an abalone boat run by his father and owned like 'everything' by the bank. We learn how Uncle Nick had disappeared in mysterious circumstances on the night of 'the crash'. This was the event that changed everything and piece by piece Parrett reveals glimpses of it through the novel. Jeff another diver is on the boat as is Martin, more an ally to Miles than Jeff and a much better person. Miles at least, knows the water and how 'not to trust it.'

3. (p11)

Back onshore Harry wakes to an empty house that has little food. He makes do with what he has and waits for Aunty Jean who is taking him to the show in Hobart, the Tasmanian capital. Harry tries not to get carsick on the way and manages to survive. Fortunately at the show he finds a twenty dollar bill and he is so happy. He ruminates on what he will spend it on, the show providing a multitude of choices for a small boy. Harry leaves his aunt at the woodchop and goes to buy showbags for himself and his brothers. He eats and then he looks at the animals before they leave for lunch in town.

4. (p23)

At lunch Aunty Jean says Harry is like his mother when he unselfishly offers to use the last of his money to buy lunch. She begins to cry and he goes to the bathroom to give her some privacy. On the way back they stop to grocery shop and we learn a little more about the poor conditions the boys live in. Harry is genuinely excited when his Dad and Miles return but his Dad has a 'headache' so Miles takes him to the bedroom. Miles is exhausted after fishing and is glad Harry will never have to 'work on the boat'.

5. (p29)

Miles is working the boat, making sure the airlines are free and working as well as positioning it. Martin surfaces and he is a man not 'like Dad'. His Dad is violent and drinks heavily while Martin seems balanced and in control. He helps Miles get sorted and then Jeff surfaces. Jeff is more like Miles' father. Miles recollects the time he had to dive and how much he hated it. Then his father surfaces with two giant bags of abalone – finally the man seems happy.

6. (p35)

Harry heads over to his friend Stuart's caravan where Stuart lives with his mum. Stuart's mum sells berries and sometimes they get to go to Huonville with her. He wanders through the bush and finds a dead bandicoot but is again distracted by a puppy that had come from 'scary' George Fuller's place. The myths around Fuller were legendary and while Harry is playing with the pup George comes out of the house. Harry runs away but hears George call his name.

7. (p43)

Joe picks Miles up at the wharf when the boat comes in so they can go surfing. Joe is sorry Miles has to go work on the boat and while they surf Joe tells Miles he is leaving in the boat he had been building for years. Joe has to get out of his grandfather's house as Jean had contested the will and won it from Joe. Joe had lived there for years but now he plans to sail the seas. Miles wants to divulge that 'things were bad at home' and he wants out too but he can't speak of it.

8. (p49)

Miles is sick when he leaves for work and Harry offers him a scarf. As Miles leaves Harry curls into the doona and thinks of the dog at Fuller's place.

9. (p51)

On the return trip in the boat they come across a school of salmon and begin to fish. A giant Mako shark chases a fish onto the boat, nearly capsizing it. The tail knocks Martin down and Jeff, who pushed Miles down to get the gun, begins to shoot despite Martin trying to stop him. Martin has to cover Miles while Jeff shoots wildly at the thrashing shark. Eventually the shark is killed but it has knocked anything of value off the deck.

Martin is injured badly, his leg obviously broken but Miles is unhurt. They now have to get Martin to the hospital and he's in a bad way. Martin warns Miles that he'll now have to work permanently and warns him to watch Jeff. Miles thinks back to when he saw his grandfather in the hospital and he was scared but Martin will recover, unlike his grandfather.

10. (p61)

Harry goes to George's to find the dog and he sees George and attempts to hide. The dog exposes Harry hiding in the bush and pulls him toward the house. George's face has been damaged but Harry can understand him when he talks. He goes into the house and they have tea while George tells him how he found Jake the dog almost dead on the road. Harry leaves but tells George he 'might come back again.'

11. (p71)

Miles has to go out on the boat the next day and, of course, Martin isn't there. It is a bad day's fishing and Miles' father is angry and heads to the pub. Miles has to 'move the boat' from the wharf on his own and then can't get the old dinghy motor to kick over. Mr Roberts tows him back and gives him a lift home. Mr Roberts had 'got rich off abalone' and tells Miles how he thinks of Miles' mother every time he passes the scene of the accident. He warns Miles not to get 'stuck here with your Dad'.

12. (p81)

Miles is ill and Harry makes him Milo but he is asleep from illness and exhaustion.

Questions on the novel

- Discuss the significance of the quote and the prologue in establishing the content, mood and tone of the novel.
- How do you see the initial sequence on the beach? Why might Parrett make this scene so prophetic? Does it foreshadow too much and is the final line 'As old as the world' too glib?
- Analyse Miles' experience with his father and his attitude and behaviour to him in this short episode.
- How do we know that the boy's home life and experiences are generally negative after the death of the mother, from Harry's breakfast and the state of the home?
- Why is Harry's finding the twenty dollars some light relief? How does the experience change his day and outlook on life?
- Why is the experience with the shark so significant for Miles and his future?
- Suggest why a mythology may have developed around a character such as George Fuller.
- Why might Harry be drawn to George Fuller and the dog?
- Mr Roberts is a contrast to the boy's father. What is his experience and how has it changed him? Why might Miles be advised to listen to his advice?
- How has the mother's accident changed life for TWO of the characters?
- List five things that might make the boy's Dad unhappy. How do his life experiences affect the way he deals with problems and how has it altered his view of the world?

13. (p83)

Lunch at Aunty Jean's was a chore for the boys as it is so pristine. After lunch she cuts their hair and Harry realises she isn't at all like his mother. We again read how she breaks down and cries. The boys hate their haircuts and Miles says, 'This is the last time.'

14. (89)

The three boys are cleaning out Granddad's house and they find parts of their mother's car salvaged from the wreckage. Miles finds a white pointer tooth in the seat and keeps it. Joe thinks that those things shouldn't have been kept. Harry just wishes Joe would stay.

15. (p95)

Harry is pleased to be going to the tip and hopes he sees a Tasmanian Tiger there. Joe tells Harry he will be coming back after his travels around the South Pacific. Harry reveals he thinks there may have been a man in the car on the night of the accident. He and Miles had been injured that night and remember little.

16. (p99)

Miles is on the beach with the shark tooth and when 'big' Gary Bones grabs it Miles chases him and gets flattened with a head butt for his troubles. Miles explains about the tooth and Gary drops it. Back home Miles is checking out his injuries and Joe gets him ice. Miles then says their mum killed herself deliberately but Joe's angry and tells him it wasn't true – she'd had a heart attack and that had caused the accident.

17. (105)

Harry awakens to an empty house and heads to George's house. He finds George down at the water heading out to fish. Harry tells him how he gets extremely sea sick so George gets out of the boat and they fish from the shore. Harry is happy and surprised that he catches a flathead. He thinks his Granddad would have taken him fishing too. He and George return to the house and cook and eat the 'delicious' fish.

18. (p113)

Miles is left to 'deal with the cannery again' and he notices that the kids he went to school with were now 'hard' men. His father picks him up late and we learn Jeff is proving to be a bad influence on his father. The two men go off poaching abalone in the afternoons. On the drive home they narrowly avoid being killed by a truck which has already mown down a bull which they spy on the roadside.

19. (p117)

George, Harry and Jake head into the bush and come to a burnt out, abandoned farmhouse where they pick fruit from a run-down orchard. It is George's old home before the fire which scarred him. Harry asks George about his parents and he tells Harry how he can remember flashes of them, especially his mother. On the way home, with two apples, Harry realises that he now considers George a 'real' friend.

20. (p123)

A car pulls into the driveway and Harry has to talk to the Fisheries officers. He learns 'Mr Steven Curren' has no fishing license and a 'long list of infringements'. The two officers leave and Harry thinks he'll go out until Miles returns.

21. (p127)

Miles has walked up to Grandad's after work and looks at the signs of his families past etched into the house. He examines the height markers 'carved' into the kitchen door and considers how Granddad 'had made beautiful things'. He recalls when he and his Granddad went to get a load of wood and how the 'huon pine' had all disappeared. Miles thinks of how the new owners of the house will think it just all firewood.

22. (p133)

Miles is watching Joe surf the 'Bone Yard' and he thinks of how Joe said he'd get 'stuck' there with all his problems. Miles, 'despite his fear', decides to risk surfing the rocks with Joe. Out on the surf he isn't scared and he is just released as he catches the waves. Afterwards they laugh and Joe tells him it's time for him to leave. He wants Miles to tell Harry he's gone. Miles just wants to escape the situation when he realises Joe is crying. Miles thinks he should be the one leaving but he thinks he will never be able to escape his life and responsibilities.

23. (p139)

Miles makes a meal for himself and Harry out of the poor fare in the house. Harry then tells Miles about 'Fisheries'.

24. (p141)

'Jeff and Dad had been drinking for two days' and the boys are scared to go out of their room. Harry has to go to the toilet and Jeff tries to force him to drink. When Miles defends Harry Jeff smashes his head into the table. Miles is bleeding and thinks about the time their father broke Joe's arm. They retreat to the bedroom and escape through the window. Harry says they can go to George's and Miles eventually agrees although he is distressed.

25. (149)

At George's they enter and he makes the two boys tea and fixes Miles' eye. The boys share a sleeping bag and the dog sidles in too. Miles enjoys the smell of George's pipe tobacco as he falls asleep.

26. (p155)

Miles dreams of Granddad and his mother picking him up to take him home. He remembers her stopping the car and heading into the trees to weep. She tells him, 'I left here once. But I came back.' They sleep late and both George and the dog are gone. They have some food, clean up and Miles says they have to go. Harry realises Joe is gone but he can't answer when Harry asks for confirmation.

Questions

- How has Aunty Jean responded to the problems the family has had?
- Why might Miles have reacted so emotionally to the loss of the shark tooth?
- Discuss why Harry is responding so positively to George.
- Analyse the decline of the father in the eyes of the boys. Refer to two specific incidents in this section.
- Describe Miles' response to Joe leaving.
- Why are the 'Fisheries' officers a problem for the family?
- Why is George so good in letting the boys stay? Do you think he knows the truth about their problems?
- What is the reason that Miles keeps dreaming about his mother?
- At this point in the novel what do you think are the TWO defining experiences in the boy's lives? Explain your response fully

27. (p161)

The boys leave George's and Miles is scared of his father so he takes Harry to Stuart's place. Miles leaves an upset Harry and drops his stuff off later.

28. (165)

Miles is back at the house and he sees a photo of his mother at 'Cloudy'. He reminisces about Uncle Nick surfing and him riding the big board. Miles then returns to reality and begins to clean the house.

29. (p169)

Dad returns with fish and chips. He tells Miles he's tuned the boat. They are to go fishing the next morning.

30. (p173)

Harry and Stuart are at the bus stop and 'Robbie Pullman's sister' who is a 'fat bitch' growls at them as they head toward the shop with Stuart's mum. Mrs Martin the shopkeeper hates kids and Harry decides to buy some expensive tea and lollies with his remaining money. The girl was still at the bus stop and Harry thinks she's 'stuck here too.' Harry gets dropped off pretending he wants to go home but once they are out of sight he turns towards George's to give him the tea.

31 (p179)

Harry finds George is not at home so he gets some wood and builds a fire in anticipation of his return. Harry sees the photo of George's brother who had died in the war and never returned. He falls asleep and awakens in the evening. Harry then decides to run home.

32. (p185)

Miles and his dad are heading home in the ute after spending all day in a heavy swell on the boat. Miles sleeps and begins to dream of his mother when the horn awakens him and Harry is in the middle of the road. Their father is angry and drives home without saying a thing.

33. (p191)

Harry is in his room looking at the sky through the curtainless windows. Miles warns him not to go back to George's as their father will go crazy. Harry agrees to stay home.

34. (p195)

Harry lies on his bed and looks at the 'Southern Lights' until he falls asleep.

35. (p197)

Their father wakes them in the middle of the night and forces Harry to go out on the boat with them. Harry gets badly sea-sick and is scared but Miles reassures him. He gives him the shark tooth to put around his neck. Outside it is cold and wet; a storm is setting in. miles helps Harry into the dinghy and onto the boat as the weather is getting quite wild.

As the sun rises Miles sees they are heading out to the 'Rocks' somewhere in the 'middle of nothing'. The men go down diving and the boys share tea and a story. Suddenly the ships pump stops and Miles can't get it restarted. Miles wants to escape as he knows his father will be insanely angry but he can't go with Harry.

36. (p207)

When his father recovers on board he attacks Miles and attempts to drown him. Miles is blacking out when he is raised up as Harry 'was going mad' attacking his father. Harry then runs to the cabin and gets on the radio telling people where they are. Their father goes insane saying the waters they are in are protected. He grabs Harry and pulls him out of the cabin back on deck. Here he sees the shark tooth around his neck and says, 'She was leaving, because of him. Because of you.' Then he pushes Harry overboard.

37. (p213)

Miles runs to save Harry but his father holds him. He admits here to moving Nick's body after the crash so that nobody would know their mother was leaving him with Nick. Miles is still his 'son' but Miles then dives down to get Harry and manages to find him in the swell and wash. He gets Harry on his back and works hard to get beyond the breaking water. Harry is scared but Miles reassures him. Miles wonders what he can do to save them.

He imagines a 'fire' and remembers when Joe had saved him in the river. He hears Harry say in a dream that he's not scared of the water anymore but in reality Harry has slipped off his back and is gone.

38. (p223)

Harry runs after Jake and at the top of the hill he can see the world. He is 'free'.

39. (p225)

Miles is in the 'orange light that came before the darkness'.

40. (p227)

Miles is rescued and it is Joe who is over him in the hospital but he reacts badly to the news that Harry is dead. Harry's body was found untouched on a reef.

Miles then goes back to the crash when the car was full of bags and Uncle Nick was in the car with them. He wakes again and tells Joe how their dad had left them injured in the car to get Uncle Nick's body away so no-one would know about the affair. He and Harry were left there cold and hurt.

41. (p233)

Joe and Miles are living on Joe's boat and they go back to the empty house. Harry's funeral is on Friday and Joe hopes their father is dead. Miles wants the photo of their mum at Cloudy. He is clearly upset and doesn't want to go to the funeral. He wants to stay away but as Joe consoles him he begins to cry.

42. (p239)

The storm has passed and Miles can feel the water in him as he looks at the sea. He heads out to surf and meets Justin Roberts who gives him a go of his new surfboard. Back on the beach he can 'feel' 'Mum and Harry' waiting but when he hears the horn calling him it's just Joe.

43. (p245)

Joe, Miles, George and Jake meet at Cloudy and they bury Harry's favourite things except for a piece of cuttlefish that Miles keeps as a memory. They go to leave and George gives Miles the shark tooth that Harry had worn around his neck. It was George who found the boy's body on the reef.

The boys leave for somewhere 'warm' and 'new'.

Questions

- If Miles is scared of his father why would he go home and clean?
- Discuss the scene with Robbie Pullman's sister. Why might she want to escape? Do you think she is portrayed sympathetically? Explain your response in terms of human experiences.
- Analyse why Harry might prefer to seek refuge with George rather than his friend? Think about why he buys the tea as a gift.
- Describe why their father might force Harry out onto the water. Does this fit into his character? Does this reinforce your opinion of him?
- Create a timeline of what happens on the boat leading to Harry getting pushed into the water.
- Why does the father blame Miles for the failure of the pump and attack him?
- What is revealed when Harry's father sees the shark tooth around his neck? How does this experience bring back other experiences and in turn affect his emotional state and behaviour?
- Discuss Miles' response to Harry being pushed overboard. How does this whole scene culminate a number of experiences?
- How have each of the characters learnt that diverse experiences and attitudes can impact on current behaviours and emotions? How do emotion and logic interplay through the decisions individual characters make? Choose TWO specific characters to develop your arguments thoroughly.
- Does any character truly learn anything positive from their experiences in the novel?

- Discuss the role of the character of George in the narrative. Does his inclusion and experience(s) add anything to the novel?
- Discuss the role of the character of Aunt Jean in the narrative. Does her inclusion and experience(s) add anything to the novel?
- Are experiences exacerbated by the concept of family and the emotions that accompany these experiences?
- Do you think the boys will return with more perspective on the events in the novel from the new experiences they will have?

SETTING

The novel is set in Tasmania and mentions many real places. Tasmania is a state of Australia off the southern coast the mainland. It is an isolated island in geographic terms and has a large wilderness area and, being an island, an extensive coastline.

The map to the right will give you an indication of the shape and main features of the island. About half a million people live in Tasmania and the capital is Hobart. Another place that is significant and mentioned in the novel is Cloudy Bay and this too is a real place below Hobart on the southern coast of the island and near Bruny Island. Setting in this manner gives accuracy and detail to the story even if the more detailed settings aren't real places. Certainly as we have read earlier the abalone industry is part of the fabric of life in this region as is the wild, cold weather which features as a backdrop to the fishing. Yet Tasmania isn't all wild and bushland as we can see from the picture of Hobart on the following page.

These websites will give you some excellent insights into Tasmania if you require more detailed information for your studies.

- *http://www.discovertasmania.com.au/*
- *http://www.about-australia.com/tasmania-facts/*

Now let's look at some of the specific settings in the novel and see how they are interwoven into the narrative. Hobart is where Harry and Aunt Jean go to the show and Harry finds the twenty dollars. It is the one of the few times we see him truly happy in the novel and the money opens up the world for him. It is a true big city adventure for the boy who lives an isolated and insecure life.

Parrett also gives us insights into the lives of the boys with detailed descriptions of the Grandfather's house, the discoveries of the babies clothes in the big wooden box in Auntie Jean's cupboard and the reaction of the Fisheries officer to the house,

'What a shithole,' (p 125)

This is not to say all the reactions to setting are negative. Miles reminisces about some of the good times he'd had at the Grandfather's house with his carpentry and the 'signs that they had been' there,

> 'Deep grooves in the floorboards in the hallways and near the doors, soot in the fireplace, brown smoke stains on the mantelpiece. Harry's treasure hunt items left hanging from the windows and resting on the sills.' (p128)

Parrett also focuses on the natural resources and beauty of the island and the way that the boys have their lives integrated into the natural world through the fishing and surfing. Even the Grandfather's carpentry shows an appreciation for the wood. We even see Harry notice that the bushland had been disturbed,

> 'And it looked like all this land had been cleared at once. A long time ago. When the forest was cleared it never looked right when it grew back. It was missing bits. There was no moss or ferns or dark hardwood trees. Just tall scrappy gums and grasses and shrubs.' (p117)

Yet it is the sea that captures our imaginations in the novel. Parrett gives it power and a unique life of its own. We see the power at the end of the storm,

> 'Boulders the size of cars had been pushed over so that the shellfish and plants living safely underneath were now stuck metres above the water, exposed to the sun. hip-high piles of kelp, ripped loose from their roots, blacked out the beach, and whole trees, leaves and all, lay battered and smashed on the rocks.' (p239)

It is the sea that takes Harry and probably absorbs their father as well. Yet at the conclusion we see Miles back at one with the water as he lets the waves roll in underneath him. We know he has survived his time in the water when most people would have drowned and he finds now the water 'felt good' as he surfs. We have also seen how the settings bring back memories for him and this is part of his experience, both positive and negative, just as the shark tooth does as an object. Miles and Joe are now set to leave and have new experiences in the South Pacific.

Questions

- Why is Tasmania the perfect setting for this particular narrative?
- Discuss the significance of 'Cloudy' to the narrative? Think about shared experiences the family have there.
- Analyse ONE of the two house settings i.e. the boys home or Grandad's house in terms of life experience? What does the house say about the people who lived in it and their experiences? What qualities should a home have? How does a house enhance or detract from experiences?
- Discuss how Hobart is portrayed and why the different environment might alter experiences.
- Describe the role of the ocean in the narrative and the lives ONE specific character in the narrative.

CHARACTER ANALYSIS

- Harry Curren
- Miles Curren
- Joe Curren
- Steven Curren
- George Fuller
- Other characters

Harry Curren

Harry carries some of the narrative in the novel and is sympathetically portrayed. When reading, you get the impression he is the author's favourite because of his naivety and general innocence in a novel where these things are precious. The youngest of the three brothers he is protected by Miles to the point where Miles feels overwhelmed by the responsibility.

While we see Harry's life as full of generally negative experiences because of his father and the claustrophobic home life we do see glimpses of happiness in his life interspersed with the negatives. Harry spends some of his time in memories and these are mostly of his mother and better times. Harry also has a positive experience with George Fuller as the novel progresses and we see him experience an adult male who has more to offer than his father. He says about George at one point,

> 'He knew they were real friends now.' (p121)

Another positive experience is when he finds the twenty dollars at the show and we see him use it to exhibit his qualities of generosity and caring, qualities that make him 'so much like his mum' according to Auntie Jean. His thoughts are to buy showbags for his brother and his friend, Stuart not just for himself despite his lack of material possessions.

Harry experiences much in his life and he sees his father's inability to cope and his anger. He is in the accident and remembers little possibly because he was injured but also because of his youth. We read how he has to fend for himself and the food supplies are often low or non-existent in the house. Harry also cannot go out to sea because he gets sea-sick and this is emphasised when his father makes him go out on the boat on that final day. Here we see Harry's insecurity,

> 'I can't go on the boat,' he said. 'I can't. Please, Miles, go and tell him? Tell Dad?' (p198)

We have already witnessed the father's intransigence and know that Harry has no chance. On the boat Harry shows his loyalty to Miles despite his size when he starts 'going mad',

> 'He was punching Dad and screaming. Screaming, 'Let him up! Let him up!' and he was kicking Dad. Kicking his legs. And Dad was just standing there laughing like it was funny...' (p209)

Harry's death that day is a significant moment in the narrative and the audience is shocked that the boy who finds joy in his little treasures that he finds along the beach could die in such a manner. The bleakness of the lives of the adults around him has impacted on such a child. Harry seems to have had so little pleasure in his life and it's suddenly over at the hand of his father. Surprisingly we see Harry still hope for rescue by his father but Miles is more aware and doesn't have the heart to tell him.

Harry dies innocent and naïve, a feat growing up in that environment.

Questions

- How do we know Harry is naïve in the ways of the world? Give three specific examples to support your ideas.
- Give one example of his innocence and state how this may be born out of his experiences.
- How do we see his relationship with his two brothers?
- List the ways in which he makes a connection with George Fuller that leads to their friendship.
- Discuss Harry's relationship with his father. Why might he think that his father doesn't like him?
- Why might Harry make a connection with George's dog?
- In one paragraph show how ONE experience shapes Harry's response to his father when he states, 'I'm glad' (p211).

Miles Curren

Miles is the middle of the three brothers and he is the father figure in the home as Joe has left. Miles is connected to the ocean and never fully trusts it, with some justification as we see in the conclusion. We read,

> 'Miles knew the water. He could feel it. And he knew not to trust it.' (p10)

Miles takes on responsibility for Harry and this is a burden that seems overwhelming at times for him. Even Mr Roberts notices and he warns Miles,

'Don't you get stuck here with your dad,' he said. Don't you let him...You're too young to be out there working, Miles. It's not right.' (p79)

Miles even feels hemmed in at times,

'He walked up the drive and thought that when he was nineteen, Harry would be nearly fifteen and they could both be the hell away from here too. That's what he thought. But it felt like it would never really happen.' (p138)

Eventually Miles gets his wish but at a great cost. He feels trapped because he is forced to work on the boat, he can't go to school and his future looks desperate. He dreams of creating furniture like his grandfather but his chances are slim. Miles is caught in the middle of two opposing forces and adding the fact he has his own personal development to undergo it is a tough time.

We see him suffer physically for his support of Harry, especially when he goes to help him when Jeff and their father are drunk. Miles is also left by the father to do what isn't his responsibility,

'Dad had left Miles to clean the boat and deal with the cannery again.' (p113)

Miles has too much and he wants to escape but it is the catalyst of his brother's drowning that breaks the cycle. After this he is able to head off with Joe to the South Pacific but we need to also consider this is more of an escape than a trip and Miles must have scars, both psychological and emotionally from his experiences,

'He listened to Joe talk about all the places they would go, the tropical islands and the clear warm water, the big bright lights of new cities. The free open space of ocean. And he knew that Joe was going to take him, now. Wherever he went.' (p237)

Miles cries after this and later they head out to Cloudy with George and Jake to lay Harry to rest by burying his little treasures in a hole on the beach. Miles thinks he'll miss 'Cloudy' but it's the only thing he will miss. Finally he gets to go 'somewhere warm' and 'new'.

Parrett uses Miles as the link between all the elements in the novel and the secret to the accident is in his memory. Throughout the narrative we get glimpses of his experiences and these reveal what has shaped his life. Miles is a balanced individual considering the experiences he has undergone and it is hard for him because of these experiences. You also need to consider how the experiences of his father help shape Miles' life and the impact of the crash.

Questions

- What in your opinion is the most significant experience in Miles' life in the novel? Support your ideas with evidence form the text.
- How do you think that the father sees Miles?
- Discuss Miles' attachment to his Granddad. What brings them close?
- Give an example of Miles' resolve to protect Harry. Why does Miles feel so strongly about his brother? Give example(s) from the text

- Choose FIVE words that you would use to describe Miles and give a one sentence supporting statement for each.
- How, through dialogue, do we see Miles' relationship with his elder brother, Joe?
- Analyse how Miles feels about his mother and the effect the mother's death had had on the family.
- What impact does Harry's death have on Miles?
- Do you see his leaving with Joe at the conclusion of the novel the culmination of his life? Think about his desire to escape the claustrophobic life he has and the level of responsibility that he has thrust upon him.

Joe Curren

Joe is the older brother and he has already moved out of home into the granddad's house because of an incident with his father. Joe's arm was broken by his Dad when he was thirteen and he hasn't been home since. Indeed the granddad left the house to Joe but Auntie Jean, 'the fucking bitch', contested the will and it is to be sold so Joe has decided to go and sail the South Pacific in the boat he has been building,

> 'Joe's boat was finished, the one he had been building all these years. It was ready to sail, ready to take Joe away.' (p46)

In many ways Joe is peripheral to the main narrative and he is more of a touchstone for Miles. They are extremely close and Miles 'wanted to stay with Joe' but he can't. The two surf together and share the same ideals. Joe is 'sorry' Miles has to work with their Dad and those two never meet in the narrative.

Joe isn't the heroic ideal for Miles though, they are more equals and friends. Miles does want to emulate some of Joe's freedom but he also wants some more. For example Joe's a carpenter but Miles wants to make furniture and be a craftsman. Joe also has moments of insecurity,

> 'And the whole time Joe looked weird and his eyes were wide and red. He looked like he was scared.' (p136)

Joe is separate from the machinations in the Curren household and thus is distanced though he isn't under any illusions as to the problems there. He certainly adds to the study of the sibling relationships in the novel and his experiences add to the impact of the main ideas that Parrett is conveying.

Questions

- How does the audience see Joe at the beginning of the novel? Does this change by the conclusion of *Past the Shallows*?
- Discuss one experience that changes Joe's view of an individual significantly. The most obvious one is with his Dad but try and think of another if possible.
- Why does Joe want to leave Tasmania? Is he right to do this in terms of his family?
- Analyse the relationship between Joe and Miles.
- List three positive experiences that involve Joe and how they impact on his attitudes and beliefs?

Steven Curren

Steven is the violent alcoholic father whose bitterness at his life and his dead wife has impacted heavily on his perception of the boys and his world. Harry's life experiences have not enabled him at all and he sinks into a world of boozy despair which ends in a seemingly inevitable act of desperate violence.

He is an abalone diver whose boat and future are lost to the banks. We read,

> 'Because the bank owned the boat now. Because the bank owned everything.' (p7)

To complicate matters the boat, the *Lady Ida* is old and at times struggles. This leads to the unfortunate conclusion when the pumps break down and Miles cannot restart them.

Steven has no paternal instinct for his boys and certainly no skills in that regard as we see how the household is run and organised. He has broken the arm of his eldest, Joe, in a fit of rage; smashes Miles' head in a drunken rage, allows Jeff to attack Harry and force him to drink alcohol and finally pushes him overboard.

The explanation for his behaviour is that his wife was leaving him for Uncle Nick on the night of the crash and that he is in pain. This seems too easy and his character must be more complex than this. Perhaps this is enough but his behaviour, in my opinion, far exceeds this and we could interpret this as he was flawed enough before the accident for his wife to leave him. Certainly he is easily influenced and when Martin is unable to work after the shark 'attack' Jeff influences him into criminal activities such as poaching and even heavier drinking. Steven never seems to be able to escape his past, especially his actions on the night of the accident. There he moves and hides Nick's body so that nobody would know his wife was leaving him. This action is more substantive to him than saving his injured boys. This shows his character clearly, himself before all else, a selfishness that is unforgiveable in the reader's eyes.

He is especially negative about Harry and there are strong suggestions that Harry isn't his child. Harry thinks his father doesn't 'like him' and Steven screams at him on the boat,

> 'You always fuck everything up. You always fuck everything.' (p210)

We can conclude that Steven isn't a very likeable character and his final actions doom him in the reader's eyes as he betrays his children and his actions lead to Harry's death. At the end we see that Miles hopes he is dead and I think most readers would see it this way. Steven's experiences in the novel are all negative and he projects this negativity onto his boys who struggle against it. Unlike them we see no positives and he allows his experiences in the past to dominate and effectively destroy his life. His escalating violence through the novel makes the reader uncomfortable as the boys have our empathy. His anger is all-consuming and directed vainly at everything. He is captured perfectly in the lines,

> 'Then they heard Dad yelling from inside. Yelling at them, at everyone. Yelling at no one.' (p146)

Questions

- How do we know from the beginning of the play that Steven Curren is basically a negative, unprincipled person? How is this reinforced as we read through the novel?
- Discuss three incidents where he shows his lack of fatherly qualities. State what each shows about his character.
- Describe his relationship with Jeff. Can we blame Jeff partly for Steven's decline?
- How does Parrett explain his behaviour? Think about the different experiences he has, the way he sees the world and how his beliefs are very different from a normal father. Do you think he is portrayed realistically or more of a caricature?
- 'Dad' is central to most of the human experiences that the boys encounter. Why might Parrett convey the most central one as a missing memory that is recounted in part until the end?

George Fuller

George Fuller is a myth around the town,

> 'Kids at school were scared of George Fuller. Harry had only ever seen him once, standing on the side of the road, but he didn't ever want to see him again. His face was all squished in and he looked like a monster...They said that George had killed his parents, burnt them alive...' (p39)

The reality is that George has been scarred in a fire that killed his parents but he, of course, isn't a monster and is more fatherly to Harry than his own dad. He is 'just a man' who is able to help the boys. George seems to know the problems at Harry's place and he offers the boy a place to find some peace and Harry becomes his 'friend',

> 'George didn't say much, but he seemed to be listening.
> He seemed to understand what Harry was talking about.'
> (p67)

George's is a sanctuary for Harry and Miles even takes him there when their Dad goes crazy with Jeff when he is intoxicated. George doesn't say much he shows what he means through actions. One such action is to teach Harry how to fish and he gives up his day on the boat as Harry gets sea sick. George is the one who finds Harry's body and he offers Miles some good advice at the conclusion of the novel as he gives Miles the shark tooth,

> 'Don't look back.'

Questions

- ▪ Discuss how the mythology could have been built up around George?
- ▪ How has the experience of the fire changed George's life and attitudes to the world?
- ▪ Analyse the relationship between George and Harry. Why might Parrett have included this in the novel when it isn't essential to the main narrative?
- ▪ Describe how the story of George's saving of Jake tells us much about his character.
- ▪ Discuss how you perceive George using specific evidence from the text to support your ideas.

Other Characters

The other characters in *Past the Shallows* highlight different aspects of the human experience. For example **Aunt Jean** has a very complex relationship with the family. She has taken the house from Joe but will put some of the money aside for the boys after contesting her father's will and winning. She tries hard for the boys; for example she takes Harry to the show, she cuts their hair and does the shopping but she is also emotionally crippled by her life experiences. We see her cry at the mention of Harry's mother and she has the baby things in the cupboard which have proven fruitless. She seems unhappy and alone. Miles dislikes her for what she did to Joe over the house but Harry is more sympathetic,

> 'He tried not to look at Aunty Jean because he knew she was crying. She wiped her face with a hankie and took a big breath.' (p23)

Aunty Jean appears infrequently in the boys lives and there is some tension that is apparent between her and the boy's father. She is the final family member we need to examine and now we can move outside the family circle and into the small community. **Mr Roberts** is a successful abalone fisherman and Miles thinks he is 'smart' having 'built up slowly' until he was very successful,

> 'He was a bear and Dad didn't like him much. No one did since he got rich off abalone, since he'd bought three new boats and built a new house and sent his kids to private school...Mr Roberts didn't care what other people thought...' (p75)

It is Mr Roberts who helps Miles at the wharf and gives him a lift home. He warns Miles to get away from his father and tells Miles 'You've had it rough enough.' He is a contrast to Miles' own father.

The deckhand and diver, **Jeff**, is everything we can dislike in a human being. Without the steadying hand of Martin on the boat after the shark accident Jeff becomes a problem for the boys. He is hard on Miles on the boat and unnecessarily cruel to Harry, especially over the drinking incident. He aids in the ethical and moral decline of their Dad without being instrumental. Jeff is always looking for the easy way and is part of the poaching and other illegal activities. We know Jeff is problematic when Martin says to Miles, 'Watch Jeff. I've tried telling your Dad but...'. Jeff is just the kind of man attracted to and attractive to a flawed human like Steve Curren.

The final people who are worth mention are **Stuart and his Mum** who play peripheral roles and highlight the tenuous grip of those on the lower socio-economic scale. No-one in the novel is wealthy except for Mr Roberts and Stuart's mum is a good example of the struggle in life with dignity. She does her best, living in the van, and providing for Stuart. She is kind to Harry and is ready to assist as best she can. She makes the best of all her experiences despite her own struggle. An example of this is when Harry describes the hot water bottles she gives the boys,

> 'Stuart was nice and staying there was good except that they had to sleep in the annexe of the caravan and the air was a bit cold on your face. But Stuart's mum always put hot water bottles in their beds so that the sheets and doona were already warm...' (p177)

Many of the human experiences in the novel are expressed through family and Stuart and his mother represent a functioning if broken one. The closeness of the community and the nature of it leave little room for privacy and we see both socio-economic struggle and personal battles with these experiences. Parrett gives us a glimpse into rural island living and the hardship of the sea through these characters.

Questions

- Analyse why Parrett includes a character like Aunty Jean in the novel. What does she contribute? Is she necessary to the narrative? Try and support your response with specific examples and evidence from the text.
- Describe how Jeff sees the world and do his experiences in the novel shape him or has his character already been shaped? Why might he be drawn to Steve Curren?
- Analyse the conversation between Miles and Mr Roberts. Why might Parrett have included this in the plot when it isn't essential to the main narrative? Why might she have included Mr Roberts at all?
- Describe what Miles' opinion of Mr Roberts says about Miles. While everyone else is jealous of his success Miles sees him as 'smart'. Consider why he might offer Miles the advice he does. For the full dialogue read pages 74–79.
- Discuss how you see 'Stuart's mum' using specific evidence from the text to support your ideas.

THEMATIC CONCERNS

- **Human Experiences in *Past the Shallows***
- **Human Experiences - Family**
- **Other Ideas in the *Past the Shallows***

Human Experiences in *Past the Shallows*

Past the Shallows is a close examination of the effect of human experiences on a family in a small Tasmanian community. We can examine the various experiences of the characters in the novel and come to some conclusions about Parrett's motivation for constructing the narrative in this particular manner. We should also bear in mind the experience of living in Tasmania that the author had and how this flavours the work. In this section I am going to focus on the general experiences that have an impact in *Past the Shallows* and concentrate in particular on the family element in the next section.

The motivations that cause many of these experiences are based in an unclear past. Harry and Miles have little recollection of the events around their mother's accident and death but through the novel other experiences begin to jog their memories. The shark tooth is emblematic of the accident and it is this symbol that draws the whole experience together, leading to Harry's death. It is the experience Miles has of getting the tooth that aids him in remembering that night and the car ride that was supposed to lead to freedom for them with Uncle Nick and his mother.

We read that the father begins his negative experience by moving Nick's body after the accident. He blames Nick for the mother's decision to leave him. He does not return to the scene to care for the boys. From here his anger and bitterness festers and his behaviour deteriorates leading to negative experiences for the boys. It is an emotionally difficult time for the boys and they get no paternal care from 'Dad'. These experiences are also physical as we see Joe's arm broken and Miles' eye split open.

Outside the family the father's behaviour also creates negative experiences for Aunty Jean and Martin and is seen by others such as Mr Roberts as a poor influence and role model. More on this in the family section but the only individual who sees their father as useful is Jeff, an individual who prefers living negatively and has a cruel streak anyway.

Certainly Parrett provides some dramatic experiences throughout the narrative. The shark experience shows the characteristics and qualities of individuals clearly – proving Martin to be a decent caring man and Jeff to be a selfish, violent figure. We see the contrast in the men in this short excerpt,

> 'No!' Martin shouted. He was trying to drag his body up and cover Miles. Don't shoo-'
>
> 'Another crack and someone was laughing. Jeff was laughing.'

Another dramatic experience is the denouement on the boat where Miles and Harry go overboard which is the culmination of all the angst that has been fermenting in the negative experiences. This also highlights the positive qualities of these two boys.

When we discuss experiences we must also focus on the small and anomalous positive experiences that we read. Think about Harry finds the twenty dollars at the show and the joy it brings him. He tells Miles away from their 'Dad' that,

'I found twenty bucks! I got you a Cadbury's bag. A Cadbury's bag! Harry held the purple bag up higher so that Miles could see it properly. I got Stuart a Redskin's bag and I got a Cadbury's bag, too, and a Redskins and a Bertie Beetle. You can share if you want.' (p25)

We can also see the joy Miles gets from his time surfing with Joe, the pleasure Harry gets from his friendship with George and Jake and the recollections Miles has of his Granddad. These are simple things that alleviate some of the darkness in their lives. These experiences are highlights that bring out strong emotions in the boys and deliver up relief for the reader from the darker elements of the novel.

The relationship with George is also a comment on how the perceptions we have change through experience and that assumptions about people can be challenged by personal experiences. Harry reflects on the reality of George's situation and his personal view which is inconsistent with his experience. Harry takes to George and finds that the myth of George held by the community is completely incorrect. He is able to alter his perception.

Parrett also focuses on collective human experiences such as the fishing trips that normally would be a bonding experience but on the Lady Ida they are basically nightmares for Miles. Compare this experience to the fishing George and Harry have on the shore that day. Harry gets a flathead then Harry is just happy to sit holding a rod in companionable silence. He reflects on the experience,

'And he thought that maybe he even liked fishing. This kind, sitting on the land kind of fishing. Maybe this was why Joe and Miles liked it so much. And he knew that Granddad would have taken him...And it would have been good like this was.' (p111)

We can examine the concepts of both individual and collective experiences when we look at the Curren family and how the influence of family shapes experiences and how people see the world. Each of the family members have both collective and individual experiences but these are perceived and acted upon differently. This is what we will examine in detail next.

Questions

- How does the smallness and insularity of the local community affect the manner in which experiences are perceived by individuals and the collective?
- Parrett shows how the local people are tied to the sea for their livelihoods. How does she do this and how is it part of their life experience? Think about how the sea shapes and influences their lives. You might also consider how Parrett makes the sea part of the local mythology with its fickle nature that Miles seems to understand.
- Discuss ONE negative experience in the novel and the effect it has on a belief or attitude.
- Discuss ONE positive experience in the novel and the effect it has on a belief or attitude.
- How does the concept of storytelling influence the content of the novel? Give specific example/s from *Past the Shallows*. Consider how personal stories such as the ones coming from the accident impact on future events and the perception of people.
- How might the experience of reading the novel change your attitudes or assumptions? You might consider the emotions that the novel evokes in you and your way of seeing characters as it unfolds.

Human Experiences - Family

The novel challenges how we see family and the conventions of what a family is. It also ponders the question of sibling attachment and examines the paradoxical nature of the father who is seemingly the opposite of what a father should be. Even the motivations for his past and current behaviour are vague and we cannot see him in any traditional manner. We can be in no doubt that the family has only dysfunctional experiences since the night of the accident and we are aware that that the family unit was breaking apart prior to that accident.

The idea that their 'Dad' moved the body of Uncle Nick to stop the other people of the community thinking she was leaving him can only be part of his motivation. She was leaving him for a reason and it is hinted at in the novel that Harry may not be his child and that she really loved Nick as indicated by the experience that Miles recalls of them on the beach at 'Cloudy'. Nick's actions which are relayed by memory certainly prove him to be more reasonable than their father. Indeed the experiences that they have with him are fond memories. We read of Miles' memory of Nick stroking Harry's cheek (p229) and of course the giving of the shark tooth.

Also of interest in this examination of the family aspect of the novel is the concept of the sibling interaction. The three brothers are of quite disparate ages and normally you'd not see the loving and respectful interactions between siblings that these boys have. We read the happy almost euphoric times that Miles and Joe have while surfing and how they enjoy each other's company,

> 'Joe was waiting for him...Everything you needed was in the van: surfboards, sleeping bags, fishing gear, tools. Miles opened the door and could smell hot chips and

gravy. There was a pile left for him on the middle seat, lukewarm and soggy but still good.' (p43)

We also get lines such as,

'He wanted to stay with Joe' (p46)

When they finally get to leave together because of the tumultuous experiences they both faced Miles and Joe are both happy. Miles excludes his father from the happy memories and at one point when he has finished surfing at the end he thinks,

'He could feel them. Mum and Harry. They were right there behind him, waiting in the Holden – Harry in the front seat grinning and telling him to hurry up.' (p243)

It is Joe in reality but these recollections sustain Miles who has had the responsibility of Harry for most of the novel. He is brilliant with Harry way beyond what you would get from a normal brother. Circumstances make Miles the genuine parent of Harry and he takes his responsibilities seriously and in turn Harry tries to do his best for Miles e.g. making him a Milo and listening to his advice. Harry even has a positive relationship with the absent Joe who cannot bring himself to tell Harry that he is leaving.

Integrated into the family experience and on-going dynamic is the persistent memory of the mother and the Granddad. These two positive memories are what the boys hang on to and both characters are well respected. It is commented that the boys, especially Harry, are like their mother and Miles wants to emulate his Granddad as did Joe in their ability and love of working with wood. The legacies of these two family members' experiences give the reader a glimpse into the ability of memory and reminiscence to influence the present and the future.

Family experiences are crucial to the development of the narrative in *Past the Shallows* and the examples in family show us how powerful these experiences are. The stifling world that the boys live in just draws them to think of escape. It happens but the exceptional circumstances that enable them to leave on Joe's boat are dramatic and need to be seen in the context of the novel's aberrant family.

Questions

- Do you get a sense of family from the Cullens?
- Discuss the shared experiences of Joe and Miles. How does this shape the manner in which they approach the world?
- What benefits are shown from belonging to a family? Are there more negatives in this instance or does Parrett have some balance?
- What problems does Miles face with his responsibility for Harry? How does this responsibility shape his life? Give specific examples from the text and one other source.
- How does the concept of memory affect the experiences in the novel? Give specific example(s) from *Past the Shallows*.
- Imagine you are Harry. How do see your brothers? Discuss whether you think that the portrayal of the siblings' relationship is realistic.

Other Ideas in *Past the Shallows*

While the main concept set for study is Human Experiences it is useful to look at some of the details of other issues that can be linked to this main theme. In *Past the Shallows* we learn that in human experiences the power of love is significant. The sacrifices that characters make for love is seen from the initial relationship between Uncle Nick and their mother through to the way in which Miles would do anything for Harry. We can also see that experience shows us that love isn't enough and the result of love can be negative although this is balanced by the way that Joe and Miles head off at the end.

Another part of the experience of the novel is Parrett's inclusion of some environmental issues. She touches on the destruction of the forests addressing the disappearance of the Huon pine,

> 'When he closed his eyes he could see it. The huon pine growing soft and silent by the rivers. The trees reaching wide out of the dark valleys, so perfect. And they would never come back like that. Not even in a million years.' (p130)

We also read of the way that once the forest is cleared it never returns to normalcy. Another issue she touches on with an environmental theme is the way that the sea is used. Their father is wanted for poaching and other issues,

> 'We're from Fisheries. Your dad's licence is not valid. Unpaid fines and a long list of infringements. We need to speak with him.' (p124-5)

We also see the father angry at Harry for using the radio and revealing their position when he is fishing in 'protected waters'.

He and Jeff have been poaching for a while and this easy way hasn't helped their situation, only made it worse.

We can also read in the novel that Parrett treats the sea almost like another character and it does seem to have a life of its own, sometimes heaving and dangerous and at other times completely calm. Often the sea reflects the turmoil on the boat and the characters state of mind. Miles seems to understand the sea while his father wants to fight and tame it. The sea has the power to alter landscape and take life – Parrett points this out clearly and yet it is also renewal. Miles realises this as he surfs and it is the sea that will take the boys away to roam the South Pacific.

You can also make the small individual experiences show how they affect people's behaviour, attitudes and assumptions. Look at the way Mrs Martin sees all school kids in her shop and Harry's genuine shopping for the tea. The kindness and mateship of Justin in the end lending Miles his new board and the kind words he offers. We can also use negative experiences such as Robbie Pullman's sister and how she is trapped there too, kicking the bus stop and living frustrated. Even small experiences have an effect on individual's lives and *Past the Shallows* does examine the minutia of experiences and people's lives.

Questions

- How does a sense of personal experience get conveyed in the novel?
- Parrett shows the significance of love in the novel. How does she do this in both a positive and negative manner?
- What is Parrett saying about the environment in the novel?
- What problems are illustrated when groups/ individuals are excluded from another group/ society. Give specific examples of experiences from the text and one other source.

LANGUAGE ANALYSIS

'There is a lyrical quality to Parrett's writing. Although told in stunningly clear—almost simple—and straight-forward prose, the story holds a poetic sensibility. Each word matters. The flow of the sentences echoes the rhythm of the ocean. Beneath the beautiful surface lies danger and risk.'

Sarah Tomp

https://www.bookbrowse.com/mag/reviews/index.cfm/
book_number/3049/past-the-shallows#reviews

Parrett's *Past the Shallows* uses straightforward prose which captures the lives of the characters she has created. They live in a small world, indeed she captures how they are trapped in that world, one of closeness and socio-economic struggle. This use of generally colloquial language makes the novel accessible to a wide range of audiences. The subject matter is also relevant with its focus on family, no matter how dysfunctional and the struggle to forge and existence and identity despite negative experiences. Parrett also manages to create characters that engender empathy and Harry is a hugely sympathetic character with his innocence and general decency.

It is Harry who is the centre of the narrative and we see much of the story from his point of view. He is symbolised by 'things' that he found and kept,

'And when Miles thought about his brother, now, it was the carefully collected shells and rocks, the driftwood and bones that mattered most. Harry's treasure hunt items that had taken up all the windowsills and mantelpieces and verandah space at Granddad's.' (p246)

Another symbolic thing is the shark tooth that is representative of another life that might have been. Uncle Nick's tooth which he gives to Miles on the night of the accident becomes a recurring motif that brings to light the events on the night of the accident. We read,

> 'A shark's tooth, cold and sharp—a perfect blade. Everything that a shark was rotted and disappeared; everything but its jaw and teeth...And it was old, the tooth. It was yellow and old and he tried to picture it around Granddad's neck, or hanging up somewhere in the shed or in the workshop...He couldn't place it. He didn't know it.' (pp99–100)

The tooth becomes more significant and we see this in the manner he defends it from Gary Bones, his passing of it to Harry for courage, the immediate hostility to it the father has on the boat and Miles' recovery of it from George at the conclusion,

> 'The white pointer's tooth come back to him.
>
> And in his mind he saw Uncle Nick get in the car. He leant over and stroked Harry's cheek. He looked at Miles...For luck.' (p250)

I have mentioned the importance of the ocean through this study guide and how it can be seen as an additional character. A review on the ABC website suggests this about the ocean,

> 'The ocean too is almost a character in the novel and it is here that we see the true character of Miles – protective, stoic and brave in the face of heavy responsibility and his father's fury while working alongside him on the abalone fishing boat; and Harry – inquisitive, generous and open-hearted yet filled with a terror of the vast, dark ocean.'

http://www.abc.net.au/tv/firsttuesday/s3261543.htm

The language, as Tomp points out in our opening quote, is simple with moments of lyrical beauty and emotion. This reflects the boy's life and as Rohan Wilson points out in *The Conversation*,

> 'It's a lesson Favel Parrett has taken to heart. The language in which she operates is so spare, so devoid of pyrotechnics, that it feels journalistic. She denies us, for the most part, even the music of rhythm and melody. Miles on the beach: "It was cloudy and overcast, but light was still reflecting off the water and it hurt his eyes."'

http://theconversation.com/an-iceberg-in-treacherous-waters-favel-parretts-past-the-shallows-6831

This language allows the narrative to flow without breaking down into sentimentality and it never over emotionalises the plight of the boys. The plot flows in a generally chronological order with some impressionistic moments and reflections of the past through memory. The writing is always connected to place i.e. the beach, the ocean, the house(s) and they reflect something relevant in the lives of the boys. Juliette Hughes in her Sydney Morning Herald review of the novel states,

> 'Parrett's writing has a real voice, with power to evoke feeling, place and character. She is capable of refreshing narrative clarity, yet at other times surprises with an intense lyricism that is never self-indulgent. Everyone is put to the test—pushed to the edge physically and spiritually in a series of events and revelations that affect not only the characters but also the reader. This book is that rare thing, a finely crafted literary novel that is genuinely moving and full of heart.'

http://www.smh.com.au/entertainment/books/past-the-shallows-20110610-1fw44.html

Parrett uses her formidable writing skills (for a first novel) to show how the experiences of the adults impact on their children. She also gives us a variety of perspectives to experiences such as the car crash and how the show the inconsistencies in human behaviour and the motivations and assumptions that flow from these behaviours.

Questions

- Discuss how the use of the ocean as a 'character' influences the course of the novel. Think about how the ocean marries to scenes and characters.
- Why would Parrett use mainly colloquial language in the play?
- Parrett uses some slang in reference to surfing and fishing in the text. Why would she keep these to a minimum?
- Parrett's language has been described as 'sparse'. Would you agree with this summation of her writing?
- Choose a reminiscence and analyse it carefully. Describe its impact on the novel as a whole and how effective it was in regard to your understanding of the experiences in the novel.
- Discuss one piece of Parrett's description and analyse its effectiveness in helping to or conveying an experience.
- How effective is the conclusion to *Past the Shallows*? Is it effective in replaying the scene of Harry collecting on the beach?

THE ESSAY

The essay consists of the basic form of an introduction, body paragraphs and conclusion. The esssay has been the subject of numerous texts and you should have the basic form well in hand. As teachers, the point we would emphasise would be to link the paragraphs both to each other and back to your argument (which should directly respond to the question). Of course, ensure your argument is logical and sustained.

Make sure you use specific examples and that your quotes are accurate. To ensure that you respond to the question, make sure you plan carefully and are sure what relevant point each paragraph is making. It is solid technique to actually 'tie up' each point by explicitly coming back to the question.

When composing an essay the basic conventions of the form are:

- State your argument, outline the points to be addressed and perhaps have a brief definition.

A solid structure for each paragraph is:
- Topic sentence (*the main idea and its link to the previous paragraph/ argument*)
- Explanation/ discussion of the point including links between texts if applicable.
- Detailed evidence (*Close textual reference – quotes, incidents and technique discussion.*)
- Tie up by restating the point's relevance to argument/ question

- Summary of points
- Final sentence that restates your argument

© Five Senses Education Pty Ltd

As well as this basic structure, you will need to focus on:

Audience – for the essay the audience must be considered formal unless specifically stated otherwise. Therefore, your language must reflect the audience. This gives you the opportunity to use the jargon and vocabulary that you have learnt in English. For the audience ensure your introduction is clear and has impact. Avoid slang or colloquial language including contractions (like 'doesn't', 'e.g.', 'etc.').

Purpose – the purpose of the essay is to answer the question given. The examiner evaluates how well you can make an argument and understand the module's issues and its text(s). An essay is solidly structured so its composer can analyse ideas. This is where you earn marks. It does not retell the story or state the obvious.

Communication – Take a few minutes to plan the essay. If you rush into your answer it is almost certain you will not make the most of the brief 40 minutes to show all you know about the question. More likely you will include irrelevant details that do not gain you marks but waste your precious time. Remember an essay is formal so **do not** do the following: story-tell, list and number points, misquote, use slang or colloquial language, be vague, use non-sentences or fail to address the question.

PLAN:

Don't even think about starting without one!

Introduce... the texts you are using in the response *Argument*: The human experience is affected by: - Idea One - Idea Two - Idea Three	You need to let the marker know what texts you are discussing. You can start with a definition but it can come in the first paragraph of the body. You MUST state your argument in response to the question and the points you will cover as part of it. Wait until the end of the response to give it!

↓

Idea One – Aspect of human experience as outlined in the textual material, e.g. physical impact. **Idea Two –** Another aspect of human experience as outlined in the textual material, e.g. psychological impact. - explain the idea - where and how is it shown in the prescribed text? - where and how is it shown in related text 1? **Idea Three** – People's sense of experience is affected by context and environment - explain the idea - where and how shown in the prescribed text? - where and how shown in related text 1?	You can use the things you have learned to organise the essay. For each one, you say where you saw this in your prescribed text and where in related text(s). Two or three ideas are usually enough as you can explore them in detail.

↓

- Summary of two key ideas - Final sentence that restates your argument	Make sure your conclusion restates your argument. It does not have to be too long.

MODEL ESSAY OUTLINE

> **To what extent are human experiences significant in the set text?**
>
> **From your studies respond to this question using your set text and at ONE piece of other textual material**

This essay needs to be attacked in a manner that responds to the question and shows ALL your knowledge about the text. The question lends itself to a close study of Favel Parrett's *Past the Shallows* as the text does show how the human experience is integral to life and how it shapes our other experiences and interaction with the world.

An introduction might be written:

> Human experiences are important in Parrett's novel *Past the Shallows* and the two related texts Lawrence's film *Jindabyne* and Ed Sheeran's song *Castle on the Hill*. These texts show how human experiences are integral to human existence and bring more meaning to one's life. Life is about experiences that challenge us and define how we see the world. They shape our beliefs and attitudes and can be confronting at the same time. Without experiences our lives would be empty and meaningless.

Your essay should then follow the outlined plan and develop these ideas. This gives you the opportunity to link the texts and fully develop each of the ideas.

ANNOTATED RELATED MATERIAL: DIFFERENT STUDIES OF HUMAN EXPERIENCES

Jindabyne – Ray Lawrence

Jindabyne is an Australian film that captures a wide array of human experiences. It touches on the ideas mentioned in the introduction to this text in a number of detailed instances. We can begin by considering the following before beginning a detailed examination of the narrative.

The collective human experience:

- Aboriginality and the spiritual;
- The Fishermen and their code;
- The reaction of the townsfolk;
- Media response;
- Interaction with the natural world.

Individual Experience:

- An individual character's response to the body – choose one;
- The killer;
- Response to the revelations;
- Past experiences and how they impact on current experiences;
- Reaction to loss – emotional;
- Assumptions about life.

We can now look at the plot to help us understand each of these issues. *Jindabyne* begins with the sound of a radio being tuned and the Australian feel of the movie is immediate with the theme music for the ABC news. Lawrence emphasises the isolation by having the radio not tune in correctly for an unknown female character, forcing her to use the cassette player. With this unusual beginning we know that her experience is not going to be positive.

We then pan to the rocks slowly where Gregory, our killer, sits patiently in a truck with the engine running watching the road. We know he is prepared for this as he has binoculars. He sees an Aboriginal girl, Susan O'Connor, driving and she is the one fiddling with the radio. He chases her down and forces her to stop. He moves toward her as we see a long shot of how isolated they are. We see his face in her window looming above her and screaming about the electricity coming down from the mountains. This film is no murder mystery, as we know from the beginning that the murderer is Gregory the electrician. This is about the experiences of the other characters in the film and how they respond to current experiences.

The Kane family, Stewart, Claire and son Tom, is waking. Claire pretends to sleep, before waking suddenly and being affectionate with Tom. Stewart and Tom head out fishing. The scene doesn't feel quite right and there is some emotional tension between Stewart and Claire that is unspoken due to what they have experienced in the past. Claire had a complicated past when she was pregnant with Tom. When she finds she is pregnant again, she becomes emotional and slightly unstable.

As the film builds we see the complex pasts of the characters and their interactions in the confinement of the small town. The fishing trip is a break from this and extremely important in their lives.

We see some of the emotional instability in characters such as Caylin-Calandria, who with Tom, has some issues at school. Along with Caylin-Calandria, Claire and Jude also have issues but in a nicely framed shot of the three female characters, we see them conform as members of a close knit group. The sacrifice they make is similar to Gregory's but on a different scale. Note the connection here and how each one is to get back to order and societal norms. This is the collective experience for all the characters.

At the Kanes' home the tensions are obvious from their past experiences but they contain it for appearances' sake. Occasionally, the tension reaches breaking point and the experience strains the superficial approach. The tension builds at home and the fishing trip seems like a good opportunity to break the cycle.

When we see Gregory dump Susan O'Connor's body in the river, we know that the fishing and her death will interact.

The next morning, the fishermen head off for their one big trip of the year and the sign 'Gone fishing' is put in the garage window. We see Billy on the phone to Elissa and putting the sign the wrong way round in the window shows his immaturity. They have already said they are taking him away to make a man of him. The four men have a few beers on the way and talk as they travel through the landscape. They intend to give Billy the experience they think he needs as a 'man' — a cultural rite of passage.

The men arrive and the high-tension electricity wires punctuate the wilderness. They begin to hike toward the valley. It's a long walk in and the terrain is hilly and difficult. They stop on the way and again we see Billy's naivety when Stewart says 'Listen to that' meaning the silence but he can't, as he has his earphones in. It is part of the break in tension of the film that they commune with nature. This experiential break affects all the men. The episode represents a distinct human experience.

Stewart wanders down the river fishing and sees Susan's body caught in the rocks. Hesitantly, he wades out to it and turns it over saying 'Oh Jesus' repeatedly. He screams for the others to come as he drags the body to the bank. He is obviously upset, making the sign of the cross. Stewart tells Rocco to 'take her, for fuck's sake, take her' and their shock is obvious. They all stare at the body and Billy goes to run off but they stop him. The four men meet and decide to leave her in the water and tie her so she doesn't float away.

The presence of the body threatens to detract from the enjoyment of the fishing experience. The act of attempted isolation of the bad experience is expected to evoke only a mild response. They do not anticipate the stormy reaction it receives when they return to the community.

The men go on fishing, with Stewart getting the first big fish on an absolutely perfect day. The lure of the fish is strong, especially when they see the big one he has caught. They have a successful and enjoyable time, a positive experience. They get a photo of the catch and Billy holds up his fish in a typical hunter/gatherer pose. Capturing an experience this way is most enjoyable.

It is a photo that will come back to haunt them as things change back in the world. An unanticipated adverse reaction can be a horrific experience.

Stewart goes to check on the dead girl, rolling her over and getting debris off her face in a quite tender gesture. The next day they head back and report it. At the car Billy rings Elissa and says they found a body but 'caught the most amazing fish'. They are told by the police to wait and seem despondent their trip has been ruined. They organise their story as Stewart says they have 'to get their story straight'.

We cut to Gregory eating breakfast and he appears to be a normal, lonely man until he goes out to his shed where he has hidden Susan's car and this reminds us of the evil in him. Consider his experience and his motivations. How does he see his actions and the world?

The next day at the station the policeman tells the fishermen 'we don't step over bodies for our recreational pursuits' and 'the whole town's ashamed of you'. When they are told to 'piss off' from the station the press are waiting for them and Billy makes a comment. Carl is angry with the press but we can begin to see signs of distress within the whole group.

The experience they had so looked forward to has become a negative one and the tensions we saw before are exacerbated by the emotional and collective response to the murder. Claire soon becomes obsessed with the whole affair because of her own state. The newspaper the next day has the headline, 'Men fish over dead body' because Billy has talked. Billy is late to work and Stewart tells him they have to 'stick together on this'.

Susan's sister calls them 'animals' and raises the race question by asking if they would have left a white girl. The Aboriginal youths begin to attack and vandalise the property of the men in violent outbursts, including throwing a rock through Billy's van window and thus endangering his baby. They insult Carl at the caravan park and vandalise the garage.

The police aren't any help and the situation deteriorates. Jude tells the police they shouldn't be enforcing the 'political correctness' laws. The intervention of the sense of Aboriginality and race challenges the assumptions people have and how we see the world. The contrasting views are ingrained in the social structures and part of different collective experiences.

The Aboriginal people see the white people as 'interfering' and the group of fishermen begin to fight amongst themselves. Elissa says they shouldn't go to the bush at all as it's sacred. The group talk about the bush and Rocco punches Stewart for saying the Aborigines are superstitious. The experience of racial tension becomes ever-present and adds to the emotional responses to the experience.

We now head slowly to a resolution of the conflict brought about by the various experiences. Each is handled in a different manner by characters and you can explore one or two of the responses. To cycle back to the original murder, Claire is stalked by Gregory in his truck. He stops her but drives off after staring weirdly, an odd experience in itself.

Terry and Stewart talk and Stewart meets Rocco and Carl. He tells them Claire's left him 'again'. Rocco can't believe it and we cross cut to her looking out into the wilderness after he looks thoughtfully out the window. These different reactions to experiences mirror attitudes in life and reactions to emotional and intellectual conflict.

In conclusion, Lawrence takes us back to the healing power of nature in our human experiences when the Aboriginal people are having a ceremony. Gregory watches while Claire walks in. Again we see his truck as an omnipresent force in the film, almost an extension of him. An Aboriginal man tells Claire to 'piss off' from the ceremony after she says she has come to pay her 'respects' but he is told to leave her alone by an Auntie.

The smoke and tribal music symbolise the ceremonial nature of the setting and the camera pans around the scene and the bush. We see parts of the ceremony with chanting and clapping sticks. The camera moves in and out while other shots pan around the bush, giving us the full experience and Lawrence portrays this as a positive, healing experience.

Eventually Stewart, Tom, Carl, Jude and Rocco arrive to pay respects. Tom runs to his mother and Stewart goes over and says 'Sorry' but is rebuffed by the father who throws dirt on him and spits, refusing his apology. Then an Aboriginal girl tells a little about Susan's story and sings the last love song Susan wrote.

The camera pans around all the faces as they listen to the song and the ceremonial smoke wafts around. It seems to have some healing effect on everyone, as it is a meaningful experience which raises the idea of the spiritual experience in the text. The girl stops singing through emotion. 'Be gone' seems to symbolise in language the whole scenario for each character.

We see a long wide shot of the bush before fading back to Gregory waiting again in his car behind the rocks for another victim. It is quite a circular conclusion and it is an odd end when he crushes the fly. We don't quite know what to make of the whole experience and he seems to be the only character unchanged by the experiences in the film.

Poem: 'Inland' by John Kinsella

The poem captures the mood and ethos of the outback farming communities and deals with the human aspect more than some of the other poems in Kinsella's collection: *Peripheral Light*. This poem is one long restless thought that mimics memories and recollection while raising the current, topical issues that concern the poet. As usual with his poems Kinsella orientates the audience early with the word 'Inland' and then continues the poem without a full stop. The poem flows with the use of commas but Kinsella allows us to stop and think with the use of the colon, brackets and the hyphen. Look for these punctuation stops as you read as they emphasise a specific point or idea that resonates with the audience.

The first stanza gives us a foreshadowing of the events to follow with the warnings in the words 'storm', 'alert' and 'uncertain'. This ominous tone is reinforced by the word 'ghosts' and the implication of death which is constant in much of Kinsella's poetry. The next stanza deals with a more human element and we get the country feel with the bracketed gossip about McHenry's accident which shows the close knit community. Habits here are formed as part of survival and known to all as we see 'the old man plying the same track' and the families possibly heading to church on the Sunday morning.

The third stanza returns to the vagaries of nature. Kinsella repeats 'uncertain' with regard to the weather. Weather and the environment play a large role in farming communities and it is especially so at sowing and harvest. Despite the uncertainty and 'ashen' days which alter 'moods', the community returns to their habits and routines which shape their lives. The next stage returns to the road and the implication of a journey but a journey that is straight and in conflict with the cycles of the natural world. The path seems already marked and measured. It is 'straight and narrow', marked by a theodolite.

The final four lines of the poem are pure Kinsella, marking the transience of humanity on the landscape. We read

> 'it's a place of borrowed dreams
> where the marks of the spirit
> have been erased by dust –
> the restless topsoil'

The European farmers had 'borrowed dreams' for their own relationship with the land but this line also harks back to the indigenous Dreamtime when the land was created. The indigenous view that the land owns the people is also true for Kinsella. This sense of nobody owning the land is strong in his poetry. European impact on the land can be seen in the spirituality being removed by the dust—dust created by the poor farming techniques transferred from a different land. He finishes with the 'restless topsoil' as if the whole earth is moving in its own discontented journey, just as the people move.

The influence here of genuinely lost spirituality and connection with the land as we move directly on the 'high road' contrasts with the more flowing, 'restless' side of the natural world. This visual contrast is obvious but we can also discuss the contrast between habit and spirit. 'Inland' is a poem that uses the landscape to show the contrast between two views of the countryside.

DRAMA: Eugene O'Neil's *Desire Under the Elms*

O'Neill sets out to instruct how the house and elms should appear and the year is 1850. Note how he describes the 'enormous' elms as,

> 'exhausted women resting their sagging breasts and
> hands and hair on its roof, and when it rains their tears
> trickle down monotonously and rot on the shingles'

and how they dominate and 'rot'. It is important to read this both in terms of the play and in the context of American theatre. The description here shows O'Neill's genius at new design and original theatricality.

Part One: Scene One

The whole first page and a third are nearly all playwright notes that describe the farm, the house and the characters of Eben, Simeon and Peter. The first words of the play, 'God! Purty!' reflect the beauty of the land and how Eben perceives it. Eben is 'resentful and defensive' and feels 'trapped' on the farm.

His older half-brothers Simeon and Peter are 'more bounce and homelier in face, shrewder and more practical.' They all have worked hard on their father's farm over the years and have little feeling for their absent father. We learn that Simeon had a 'woman' who died and that Peter is excited by the prospect of 'gold in the West'. They all talk about how hard they've worked and hope that the father might 'die soon'. What we get from all this is that they are earthy and this is reflected in their bodies and clothes which are all dirt stained.

We also see here the difference between them as Eben sees gold in the pasture, not California, as they head in for a dinner of bacon in what seems a ritual they have performed many times before. Note that O'Neill calls for the use of the curtain at the end of the scene.

Scene Two

It is twilight and again we get detailed notes on the interior scene. Simeon tells Eben he should not wish their father dead and Eben replies he's not his son but, 'I'm Maw – every drop of blood!' He then blames the father, Ephraim Cabot, for killing his mother by working her to death but the others just say there was work to be done. O'Neill gets them to list the jobs and Eben comes back with 'vengeful passion' that, while they did nothing, he will see his mother gets 'rest and sleep in her grave!'

They then discuss Cabot's absence and how he just drove off in a buggy one day in a rush. Simeon says that when he went,

> 'He druv off in the buggy, all spick an' span, with the mare all breshed an' shiny, druv off clackin' his tongue an' wavin' his whip. I remember it quite well'

Eben mocks Simeon for not stopping him and the scene concludes with Eben leaving to see Minnie the town whore. We learn all the Cabot men have slept with her. Simeon and Peter say that Eben is just like 'Paw' and thinks of California. The final image is of Eben with his arms stretched to the sky talking about starts and sin, 'my sin's as purty as any one on 'em!', until he 'strides' to the village for Min.

Scene Three

It is 'pitch darkness' and Eben comes home with the news that Cabot has married a 'purty' thirty-five year old. He has heard this in the village and this effectively disinherits the boys. Simeon and Peter see California as their only option now. Eben tells the boys that they can have three hundred dollars each if they sign their share of the farm over to him. He can get the money as his mother told him,

> 'I know whar it's hid. I been waitin' – Maw told me. She knew whar it lay fur years, but she was waitin'....It's her'n – the money he hoarded from her farm an' hid from Maw. It's my money by rights now.'

They think about it and Eben tells them about his night with Min. He tells how he hates the new wife after the boys suggest he might sleep with her, just like Min, to get the old man back. Peter and Simeon say they'll do the deal and leave the farm. Both are bitter and vindictive about Cabot.

Scene Four

The setting is the same as Scene Two and the boys are discussing how they don't have to work now – it is all down to Eben who is jubilant as he thinks it will all be his. Peter and Simeon again reflect on how like his father he is, 'Like his Paw'. They also tell he isn't much of a milker but they soon talk about their leaving and how they'll miss some aspects of the farm.

Eben comes back in and says that the 'old mule an the bride' are coming. The two older boys begin to pack and sign Eben's papers as he gives them the money Cabot had hidden. They tell him they'll send him 'a lump o' gold for Christmas' and head into the yard feeling 'light' because of their newfound freedom.

Ephraim Cabot and Abbie Putnam then come in and O'Neill describes them in detail. Cabot is

> 'seventy-five, tall and gaunt, with great, wiry, concentrated power, but stoop shouldered by toil. His face is hard as if it were hewn from a boulder, yet there is a weakness in it'

but his face is weakened with petty pride. Abbie is

> 'thirty-five, buxom, full of vitality. Her round face is pretty but marred by its rather gross sensuality. There is strength and obstinacy in her jaw, a hard determination in her eyes, and about her whole personality.'

She also has a 'desperate quality'. Cabot shows Abbie the place and she says to him it's 'mine'. Then he sees the two boys not working. He introduces Abbie and she goes to look at 'her' house and they warn her Eben's inside.

Cabot tells them to get to work and they give him cheek, saying they are 'free' and heading to California. They 'whoop' it up and he says he'll have them chained up. They throw rocks at the house, smashing the window and head off singing. Abbie sticks her head out the window and says she likes the room but he is thinking of the stock and 'almost runs' to the barn.

Abbie then meets Eben in the kitchen and talks to him in 'seductive tones'. She says she doesn't want to be his 'Maw' but friends and he cusses her. She tells him of her troubled life and how Cabot gave her a chance to escape it. He calls her a 'harlot' and they argue over ownership of the farm. She has the upper hand in law and he leaves but the seeds of their growing attraction have been set.

Outside he and his father argue about life and work and he tells Eben 'Ye'll never be more'n half a man!' The scene ends with Abbie washing up and the faint notes of the song the boys were singing as they left.

Part Two: Scene One

Again O'Neill describes in detail the farmhouse setting. Two months have passed and it is a hot Sunday afternoon. Abbie in her best outfit is sitting on the porch and Eben comes out of the house also dressed in his best. They stalk each other, both attracted and repelled. As he walks away she 'gives a sneering, taunting chuckle' at him and they argue but the attraction is obvious. She says that nature will pull him to her but he says that she is married and he goes to leave her.

She accuses him of going to Min and she gets angry stating he'll never get the farm,

> 'Ye'll never live t' see the day when even a stinkin' weed on
> it 'll belong t' ye!'

He says he hates her and leaves as Cabot enters. She tells him Eben has been mocking him and twists the conversation to the inheritance of the farm. She tells him Eben lusts after her and as he angers she backs off in her accusations. Reassured, he says that she can have the farm if she bears the son she says she wants with him. He says that he'd 'do anythin' ye axed, I tell ye!' if she gave him a son and tells her to pray to God for it to happen.

Scene Two

It is about eight in the evening and here the bedrooms are highlighted, with Eben in one and Cabot with Abbie in the other. The two of them are talking about a son. They seem together, yet apart, as he tells her of his life on the farm and how God's hard. He both lost and gained on the way through, but the farm is his. He says he is pleased he found her, his 'Rose o' Sharon'. Abbie promises him that she will bear a son as he basically threatens her,

> 'Ye don't know nothin' – nor never will. If ye don't hev a son t' redeem ye...'

and he leaves to sleep in the barn with the cows 'whar it's restful'.

We then see Eben and Abbie restless and she leaves the room and goes to him. He 'submits' to her kisses then 'hurls' her away. Abbie says she'd make him 'happy' and she knows he wants her too much. She tells him to go down to the parlour and he is shocked as this is where his mother was 'laid out'. She leaves for the parlour and he wonders what's happening. The scene closes with a question to his dead mother, 'Maw! Whar are yew?' but we know that he wants her and will go to her.

Scene Three

The scene now shifts to the parlour which is described as a 'grim, repressed room like a tomb'. Abbie waits and Eben appears and he sits at her invitation. They talk about his Maw and how they hate Cabot. Abbie throws herself at him with 'wild passion' and he is caught up in the moment and thinks that it's his Maw wanting him to sleep with Abbie to get revenge on Cabot,

I see it! I sees why. It's her vengeance on him – so's she kin rest quiet in her grave!

Abbie proclaims her love for him and he for her then they kiss 'in a fierce, bruising kiss' to close the scene.

Scene Four

A more bold and confident Eben leaves the house and Abbie opens the parlour window. She calls him over for a kiss and they talk a bit before Eben says his Maw can now rest. They split as Cabot comes out of the barn but are now obviously in love. Eben tells Cabot that his Maw is now at rest and Cabot says he rests best with the cows. Cabot is confused but the scene ends with him criticising Eben as 'Soft-headed' and a 'born fool' but, being a practical man, he heads for breakfast.

Part Three: Scene One

Time has passed to 'late spring the following year'. Eben is upstairs in emotional and psychological conflict while a party happens downstairs. Cabot has drunk too much and Abbie sits, pale and thin, in a rocking chair. There is a fiddler and Abbie begins the scene by asking for Eben and the guests 'titter' as most think the baby is Eben's, not Cabot's, which is true enough. They laugh and Cabot is angered by this and orders them to dance. The fiddler 'slyly' says they're waiting for Eben but Cabot mocks the boy and then ensues a bawdy conversation about his fertility,

I got a lot in me – a hell of a lot – folks don't know on. Fiddle 'er up, durn ye! Give 'em somethin' t' dance t!'

The fiddler plays and they dance. Cabot joins in frantically and 'whoop(s)' it up. He exhausts the fiddler and pours whiskey. In the upstairs room Eben is looking at the baby. Abbie goes upstairs and Cabot leaves for outside, 'fresh air', as she has told him not to 'tech' her. The guests gossip after he goes and we see Eben and Abbie upstairs and she professes her love for him,

'Don't git feelin' low. I love ye, Eben. Kiss me.'

Cabot says he's going to rest in the barn. The scene concludes with the fiddler playing in celebration of 'the old skunk gittin' fooled!'

Scene Two

Eben is outside half an hour later and Cabot is coming back from the barn. Cabot tells him to get a woman inside and he might get a farm. Eben replies that this farm's his and Cabot mocks him. He tells her Abbie has been promised the farm for her son and Eben is angered thinking Abbie has tricked him.

Eben goes to kill her but Cabot is too strong for him and Abbie comes out to stop him choking Eben. Cabot tells him he's weak and goes inside to celebrate. Abbie tries to be tender with Eben but he rejects her and calls her a liar.

'Ye're nothin' but a stinkin' passel o' lies. Ye've been lyin' t' me every word ye spoke, day an' night, since we fust – done it. Ye've kept sayin' ye loved me....'

She says she loves him and tells him that the promise was made before they fell in love. He says he'll go to California.

They argue and he 'torturedly' says he wished the baby had never been born. Abbie is distraught and she says she'd kill the baby to prove her love for him. He says he won't listen to her but she calls after him that she can 'prove' she loves him and she 'kin do one thin' God does'. Abbie is desperate at the end of the scene.

Scene Three

It is now just before dawn and Eben is in the kitchen ready to leave. Abbie is near the cradle with 'her face full of terror'. She sobs but Cabot stirs and she goes to the kitchen and flings her arms around Eben, kissing him 'wildly'. She says 'I killed him' and he thinks she means Cabot but is horrified when she tells him it's the baby.

Eben states it was his baby and she says she loved it but loves him more. He is angered,

> 'Don't ye tech me! Ye're pizzen! How could ye – t' murder
> a pore little critter – Ye must've swapped yer soul t' hell!'

and tells her that he is getting the Sheriff and heads, 'panting and sobbing' to town. She calls out to him that she loves him.

Scene Four

It is after dawn and Abbie is in the kitchen. Cabot wakes in his room and is concerned that he has woken late. He checks the baby and is proud it is quiet and asleep. He goes down to Abbie in the kitchen and she tells him the baby is dead. He runs to check and comes back down and asks 'why?'

In a rage she tells him it was Eben's son and that she loves Eben, not him. He blinks back a tear and then gets 'stony' so he can carry on and says he is going to get the Sheriff. Abbie tells him that Eben's already gone so that Cabot tells her he'll 'git t' wuk.' He then tells her he'd never have told and now he's going to be 'lonesomer'n ever!' Eben comes back and Cabot tells him to get off the farm.

Eben asks for her forgiveness and tells her he loves her. He says he realised he loved her at the Sheriff's and they have a chance to run away but Abbie says she'll take her punishment. Eben says he will share it with her and plans to tell the Sheriff they planned it together. They think they can stand it together and then Cabot comes back.

He goes into a long tirade and tells them how he's let the stock go and will burn the house down. He too plans to go to California but finds that Eben has gotten to his money first. Cabot says that this is a sign from God to him to stay and that 'God's hard an' lonesome!' At this point the Sheriff comes and Eben says he was involved with the baby's murder.

Cabot says 'Take 'em both' and leaves to get his stock. The sun is coming up and as they are led away Eben says the farm's 'Purty' and Abbie agrees. The Sheriff finishes the play with the line, 'It's a jim-dandy farm, no denyin'. Wish I owned it!'

OTHER RELATED TEXTS

Fiction / Non-fiction / Drama

- *Wonder* – R G Palacio
- *First they Killed My Father* – Luong Ung
- *The Graveyard Book* – Neil Gaiman
- *Looking for Alaska* – John Green
- *Eleanor and Park* by Rainbow Rowell
- *The Fault in Our Stars* – John Green
- *We All Fall Down* – Robert Cormier
- *The Old Man and the Sea* – Ernest Hemingway
- *The Fire Eaters* – David Almond
- *Ender's Game* – Orson Scott Card
- *Hatchet* – Gary Paulsen
- *Inside Black Australia* – Kevin Gilbert
- *Sapiens: A Brief History of Humankind* – Yuval Noah Harari
- *Peeling the Onion* – Wendy Orr
- *Raw* – Scott Monk
- *Six Degrees of Separation* – John Guare
- *The Book Thief* – Markus Zusak
- *When Dogs Cry* – Markus Zusak
- *Holes* – Louis Sachar
- *The Outsiders* – S.E. Hinton
- *Roll of Thunder, Hear My Cry* – Mildred D. Taylor
- *A Small Free Kiss in the Dark* – Glenda Millard
- *Monster* – Walter Dean Myers
- *Lord of the Flies* – William Golding
- *Jandamarra* – Steve Hawke
- *A Separate Peace* – John Knowles
- *A Monster Calls* – Patrick Ness
- *The Pigman* – Paul Zindel
- *The Invention of Hugo Cabret* – Brian Selznik

- *Emerald City* – David Williamson
- *Silent Spring* – Rachel Carson

Films and Television

- *The Human Experience* – Charles Kinnane
- *My Brilliant Career* – Gillian Armstrong
- *Broadchurch* – James Strong & Euros Lyn
- *Twinsters* – Samantha Futerman and Ryan Miyamoto
- *Be My Brother* – Genevieve Clay - Smith
- *What's Eating Gilbert Grape* – Lasse Hallstrom
- *Pleasantville* – Gary Ross
- *Eternal Sunshine of the Spotless Mind* – Michel Gondry
- *Taxi Driver* – Martin Scorsese
- *Tootsie* – Sydney Pollack
- *Back in Time for Dinner* – Kim Maddever
- *The Godfather* – Francis Ford Coppola
- *Friends* – David Crane and Marta Kaufmann
- *Dawson's Creek* – Kevin Williamson
- *Orange is the New Black* – Jenji Kohan
- *Boy Meets World* – Michael Jacobs and April Kelly

Website – quote on literature and the human experience

http://view2.fdu.edu/academics/university-college/school-of-humanities/
english-language-and-literature-program/

At its most fundamental level literature explores what it means to be a human being in this world and tries to describe what our human experience is like. As such, literature pushes us to confront the large human questions that have plagued humankind for centuries: issues of fate and free will, issues relating to our role in the universe, our relationship to God, and our relationships with others. Studying literature not only helps us to understand the complexity of these questions intellectually, but because of its very nature, it allows us to experience these tensions vicariously. Literature does not just tell us about human experience; it recreates it in a way we can feel and visualise. In other words, it calls for a total response from us—it stretches us beyond who we are.

First, literature can enhance our ability to relate to people. Because literature focuses on human relationships and self perception, it can broaden our own experience—to help us understand different kinds of people, different cultures, different problems—and, consequently, help us better understand our own relationships with others.

The study of literature also helps to foster an appreciation for beauty, symmetry, and order. This means more than the intuitive response of liking or disliking something we see or read or hear; it means a carefully thought-through response that will enhance appreciation—not destroy it.

Perhaps the most important skills that the study of literature teaches are analytic and synthetic skills. In learning to read carefully and analytically, we learn to ask hard questions both of the work and of ourselves. And as we seek to discover the relationships between the ideas and images we uncover in a work, our ultimate goal is to see the whole—to see how the parts work together to make the piece what it is. In grappling with the complex and difficult ideas contained in literature, we learn to accept the multiple dimensions and ambiguity that are so often present in life.

Finally, the study of literature will also help develop our writing abilities as we come to value the written word and understand its power to communicate.

Beyond all of these skills, however, it is not what literature can do for us as individuals as much as what it can do to us. Literature speaks to the whole person. Listen to it, says C. S. Lewis, and you will be changed.

Poetry

- 'Warren Pryor' – Alden Nowlan
- 'The Gardener' – Louis MacNeice
- 'The Improvers' – Colin Thiele

Songs

- *Be My Escape* – Relient K
- *Mandolin Wind* – Rod Stewart
- *Roxanne* – The Police
- *Wake Me Up When September Ends* – Green Day
- *Under Pressure* – Queen & David Bowie
- *Candle in the Wind* – Elton John
- *Empire State of Mind* – Alicia Keys
- *Gold Digger* – Kanye West
- *We Are Young* – Fun.
- *Centrefold* – J. Geils Band
- *It's Time* – Imagine Dragons
- *We Cry* – The Script
- *If I Were a Boy* – Beyoncé
- *Shake it Out* – Florence + the Machine
- *C'mon* – Panic! At the Disco & Fun.
- *I Don't Love You* – My Chemical Romance
- *Sing* – My Chemical Romance
- *1985* – Bowling for Soup
- *What About Me* – Shannon Noll
- *Sinner* – Jeremy Loops
- *7 Years* – Lucas Graham

- *Bitter Sweet Symphony* – The Verve
- *Ghost!* – Kid Kudi
- *Good Riddance (Time of Your Life)* – Green Day
- *Expectations* – Belle and Sebastian
- *After Hours* – We Are Scientists
- *Write About Love* – Belle and Sebastian
- *Trust Your Stomach* – Marching Band
- *Heaven Knows I'm Miserable Now* – The Smiths